HELLO NATURE

BELONGS TO

Nina Chakrabarti

HELLO NATURE

DRAW, Color, MAKE, and GROW

LAURENCE KING PUBLISHING

A catalog record for this book is available
from the BRITISH LIBRARY.

ISBN : 978-1-78067-735-4

Printed in China

FOR Ben Branagan

'...WHEREVER YOU ARE and
          WHATEVER YOUR RESOURCES,
YOU CAN STILL LOOK UP at THE SKY—
     its DAWN and TWILIGHT BEAUTIES,
ITS MOVING CLOUDS, its STARS by NIGHT.
...PONDER the MYSTERY
          of A GROWING SEED...
PLANTED in A POT OF EARTH
          in THE KITCHEN WINDOW.'
                    — Rachel Carson
          SCIENTIST, WRITER, and ECOLOGIST
                    1907-1964

PLANET EARTH

(A.K.A. HOME)

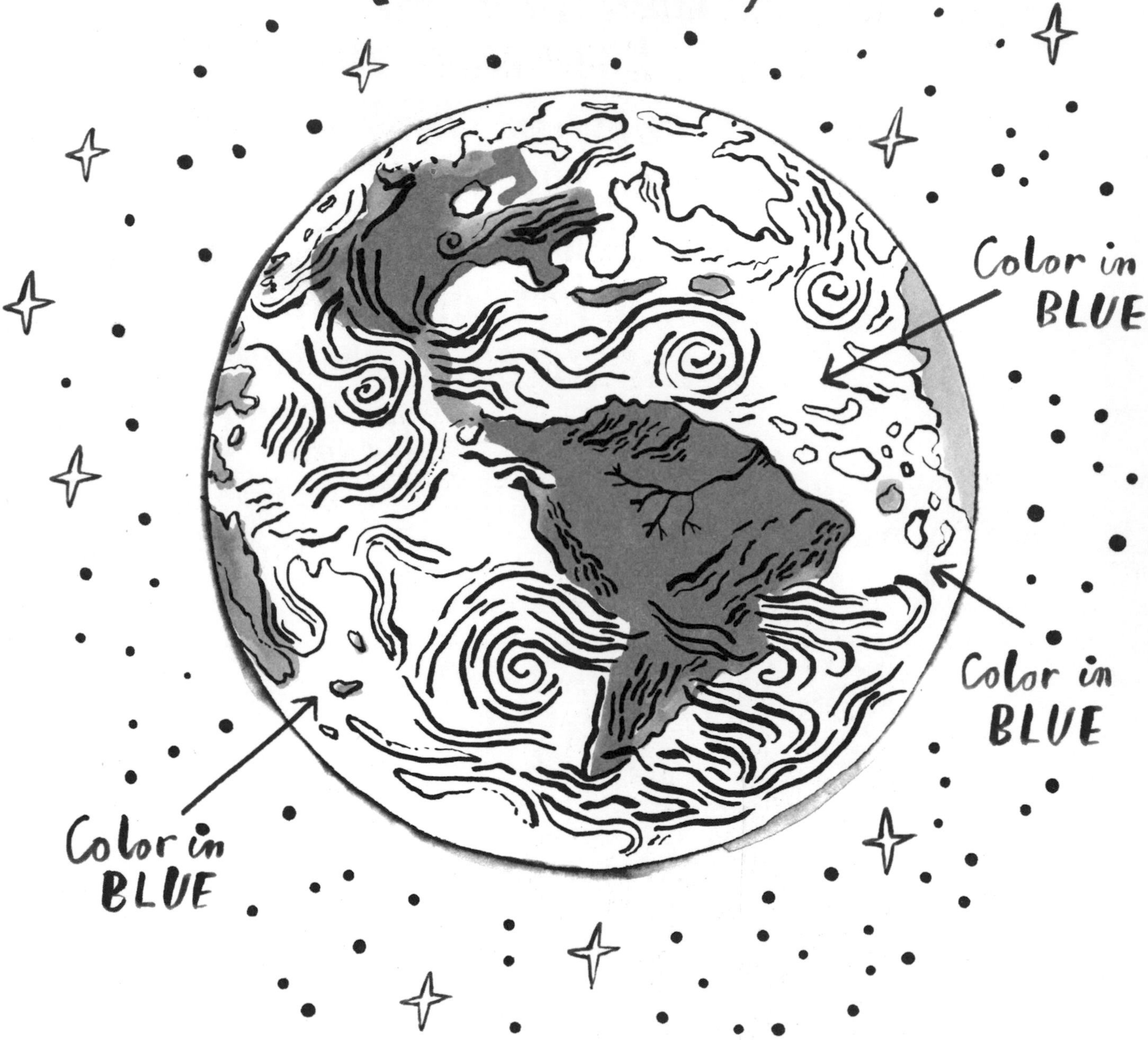

SOMEWHERE on THIS PLANET
IS YOU

EARTH is FOUR and A HALF BILLION YEARS OLD
How old are you?

DRAW YOU AT THIS
PRECISE MOMENT IN TIME

CELEBRATE our NEAREST STAR
Without THE SUN there would be NO life on earth

MAKE a SUN MASK

Design YOUR OWN SUN MASK
on this page

Think SUNNY THOUGHTS!

TRY a SUN EXPERIMENT

① Use both these PAGES to DRAW the HORIZON
outside your home

② Mark where the SUN RISES and SETS
using DIFFERENT colored DOTS

③ After a couple of MONTHS you will see how the DOTS MOVE across the PAGE!

* Remember: STAND in the same SPOT each time OTHERWISE your SUN RECORD will NOT be ACCURATE

Draw the MOON'S CRATERS, VALLEYS, and SEAS

Look at the MOON through BINOCULARS or a TELESCOPE

'A most beautiful and rapturous sight to behold'
—Galileo Galilei
THE FIRST PERSON TO MAKE PROPER MAPS OF THE MOON

OUR MOON

It's faraway, GRAY and has
NO ATMOSPHERE BUT
it's still VERY magical
to LOOK AT from earth

WRITE a song or poem about the moon
ON this PAGE

Hyacinths

GROWING SPROUTS

Tadpoles and Chicks

GALOSHES and UMBRELLAS   CROCUS

WORMS **HELLO** BUDS

EGGS HATCHING

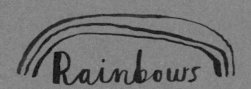
Rainbows

BUTTERFLIES and MOTHS

Herbarium making—   BIRDSONG

ROBINS and BLACKBIRDS

NEST BUILDING

PLANTING SEEDS

LEAVES GROWING

SNOWDROPS

Cherry Blossom

SPRING

RABBITS

Flower Pressing

MELTING SNOW

DAFFODILS and BLUEBELLS

SUNSHINE and SHOWERS

IDENTIFY TREES by their LEAVES

WEEPING WILLOW

DOUGLAS FIR

GINKGO BILOBA

COMMON ASH

SUGAR MAPLE

TULIP or WHITEWOOD

FIG

ENGLISH OAK

They GROW in twinkling clusters and can cover 3 FEET or MORE with their TRAILING stems

DRAW the missing VEINS on these NASTURTIUM leaves

DRAW your DREAM TREE HOUSE
on this page

WHAT DOES the INSIDE OF YOUR TREE HOUSE LOOK LIKE?

herbarium:
NOUN
1. a systematically
arranged collection
of dried plants

The POET and lifelong gardener
EMILY DICKINSON made
a book full of dried plants
and flowers as a 14 year old

Emily Dickinson
1830~1886

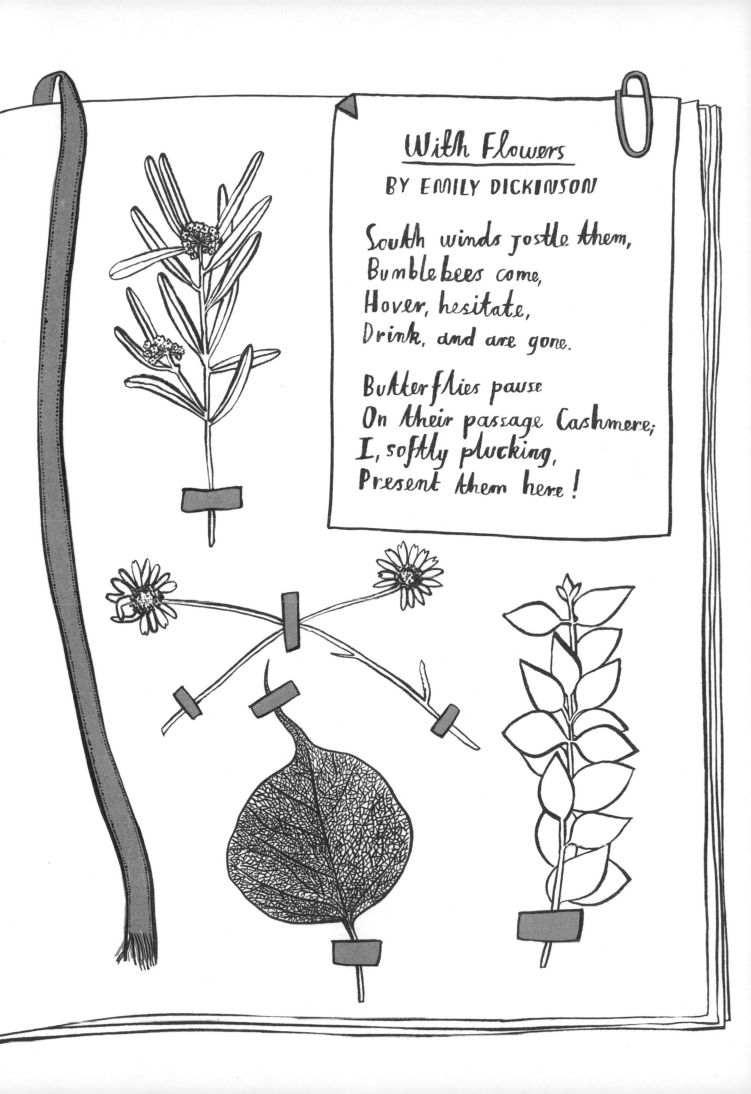

With Flowers

BY EMILY DICKINSON

South winds jostle them,
Bumblebees come,
Hover, hesitate,
Drink, and are gone.

Butterflies pause
On their passage Cashmere;
I, softly plucking,
Present them here!

MAKE your OWN HERBARIUM

You will need: PRUNING SHEARS ——→
(THESE ARE SCISSORS FOR PLANTS)
STICKY tape CUT INTO STRIPS
SKETCHBOOK or NOTEBOOK
PLANTS: Flowers, Leaves, Petals
LABELS

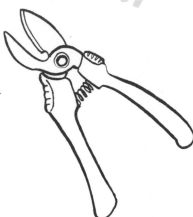

① LOOK in YOUR GARDEN FOR PLANTS you WOULD LIKE to PRESS

② USING your PRUNING SHEARS, CUT the SPECIMENS CAREFULLY and PLACE BETWEEN SHEETS of NEWSPAPER

③ PLACE between THE PAGES OF a BOOK (YOU CAN USE THIS ONE IF THE PLANT WILL FIT) AND WEIGH DOWN with SOMETHING HEAVY

④ NOW it NEEDS to BE LEFT alone FOR 3-5 DAYS SO the PLANT can DRY OUT

⑤ WHILE the PLANT is DRYING OUT, CREATE a BEAUTIFUL COVER for YOUR HERBARIUM

⑥ **FILL** in **ONE OF** the **LABELS LISTING WHERE** you **PICKED YOUR PLANT,** the **DATE,** and **SCIENTIFIC NAME**
(LOOK THIS UP IN A BOOK IF YOU DON'T KNOW)

⑦ **WHEN COMPLETELY** dry, **LIFT** out **THE PLANT SPECIMEN** and **PLACE** in **YOUR NEWLY** transformed **NOTEBOOK**

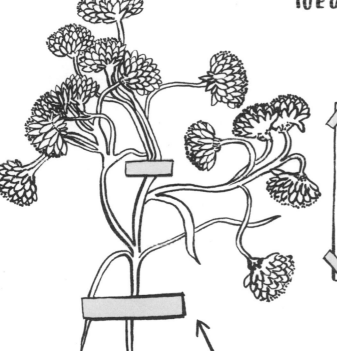

Date: THE DAY, THE MONTH, THE YEAR
Name (scientific): THE PLANT'S LATIN NAME
Name (common): THE PLANT'S MODERN NAME
Location: WHERE YOU FOUND THE PLANT
Notes: COLOR? SMELL?
ANYTHING ELSE?

⑧ **USE** the **STRIPS** of **STICKY TAPE** to **FIX THE PLANT** to **THE PAGE** and **STICK THE** label **NEXT** to **IT**

⑨ **KEEP COLLECTING UNTIL** you **FILL UP YOUR HERBARIUM**

⑩ **NOT** only **ARE YOU COLLECTING** little pieces **OF NATURE** and **LEARNING ABOUT PLANTS, BUT ALSO** in **YEARS** to **COME YOUR BOOK WILL** be **FULL OF MEMORIES**

Fill these PAGES with LOTS of SPRING FLOWERS

SNOWDROP
SPOTTED
27th FEBRUARY

PANSIES, SNOWDROPS, DAFFODILS, BLUEBELLS, and CAMELLIAS are a few OF MY FAVORITES

What are YOURS?

HOW to TELL THE DIFFERENCE BETWEEN FROGS and TOADS

FROGS like TO LIVE NEAR WATER

PAINT the FROGS USING BRIGHT COLORS

SMOOTH, slimy SKIN

LONG legs for JUMPING

FROGS lay EGGS in big, LUMPY CLUMPS

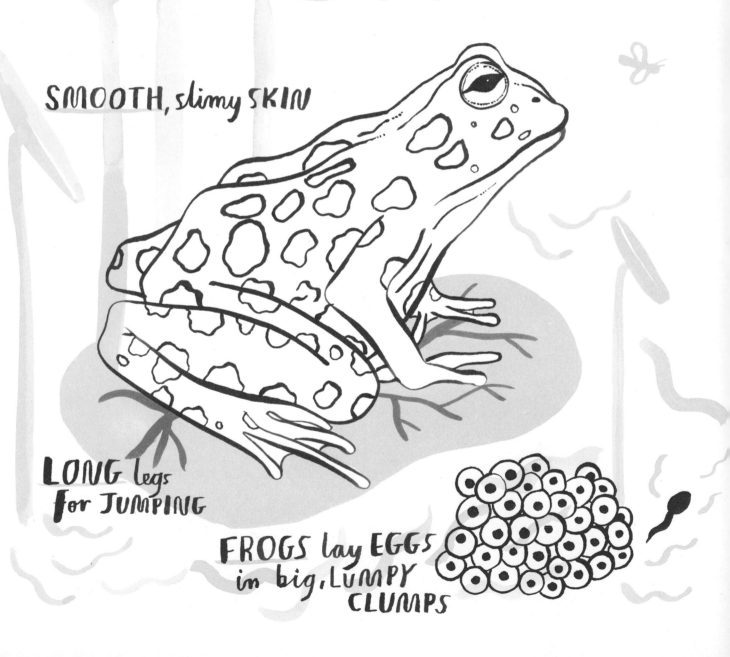

COLOR the TOAD
USING DARK, MUDDY HUES

TOADS can LIVE on LAND and PREFER a DRY CLIMATE

VENOM GLANDS BEHIND the EARS (FROGS DON'T HAVE THESE)

BUMPY, dry SKIN

SHORT HIND LEGS FOR WALKING and short HOPS

TOADS lay eggs IN a CHAIN

DRAW Lots of TADPOLES
swimming in this LILY POND

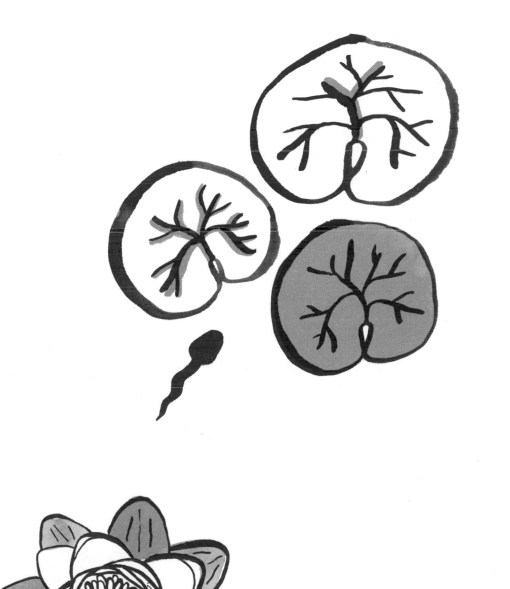

Toads LOVE to EAT all KINDS of INSECTS and WORMS

In SUMMER, a TOAD can EAT as many as
- 1000 - insects a DAY

Fill this PAGE with TOAD FOOD

Draw ants, EARTHWORMS, CENTIPEDES, DRAGONFLIES, beetles, GNATS, SPIDERS, CRICKETS, GRASSHOPPERS, flies, and ANY OTHER CREEPY-CRAWLIES YOU can THINK OF

DRAGONFLIES HAVE TWO PAIRS of WINGS that STICK OUT FROM THEIR BODIES

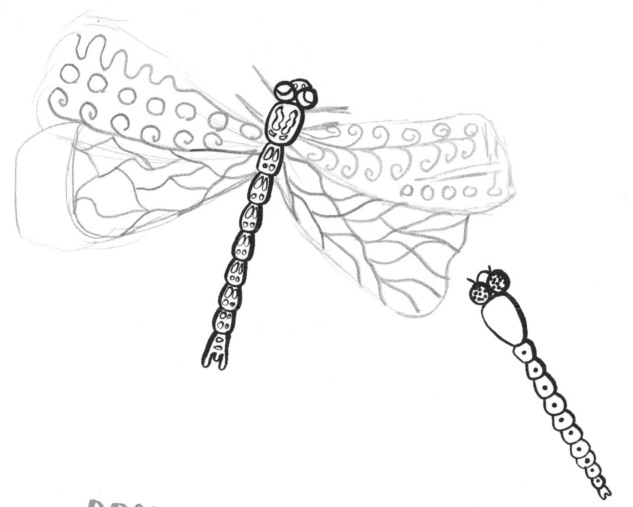

DRAW the WINGS ON TO these DRAGONFLIES

DRAW a FROG JUMPING
FROM this LILY PAD
Wheeeeeeeee!

DRAW a TOAD sticking
out its LONG TONGUE and
EATING LOTS of BUGS

HOW to TELL THE DIFFERENCE BETWEEN a MOTH and A BUTTERFLY

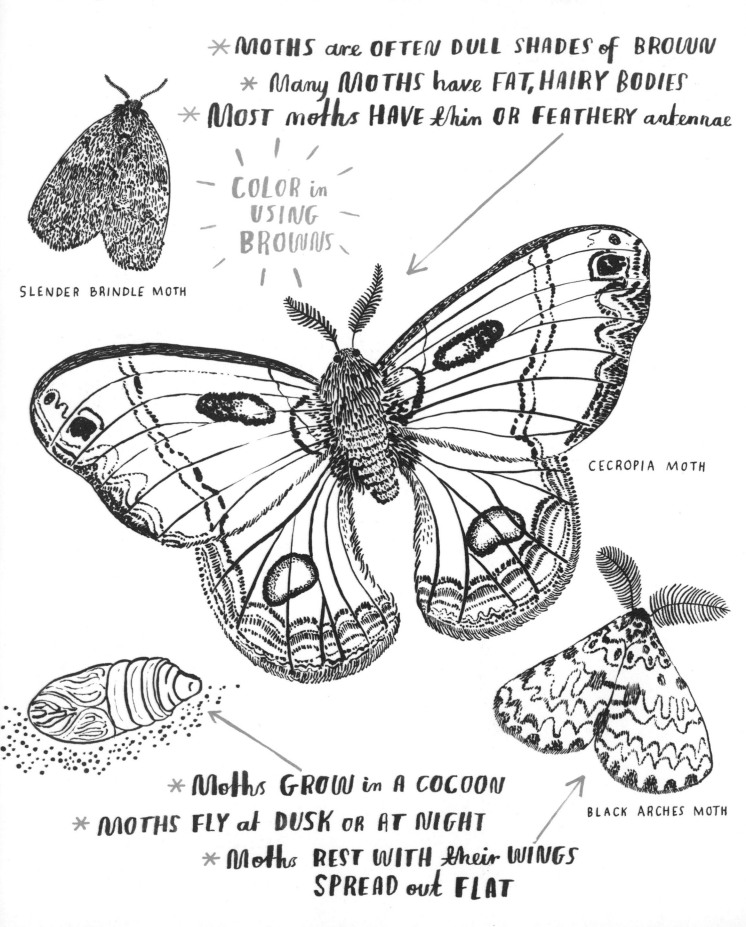

* MOTHS are OFTEN DULL SHADES of BROWN
* Many MOTHS have FAT, HAIRY BODIES
* MOST moths HAVE thin OR FEATHERY antennae

COLOR in USING BROWNS

SLENDER BRINDLE MOTH

CECROPIA MOTH

BLACK ARCHES MOTH

* Moths GROW in A COCOON
* MOTHS FLY at DUSK OR AT NIGHT
* Moths REST WITH their WINGS SPREAD out FLAT

* Butterflies HAVE CLUBBED, thread-like ANTENNAE
* BUTTERFLIES have SLENDER, hairless BODIES
* Butterflies TEND to BE COLORFUL

THE RED POSTMAN

ADONIS BLUE

COLOR in USING REDS, blues, AND YELLOWS

SWALLOWTAIL

* BUTTERFLIES grow IN A CHRYSALIS
* BUTTERFLIES fly DURING THE day
* Butterflies USUALLY rest WITH THEIR wings UPRIGHT

The butterfly counts not
months BUT moments,
and has time enough.
— Rabindranath Tagore

INDIAN POET, PHILOSOPHER, and ARTIST

COLOR IN *these*
MAGNIFICENT MOTHS

SCALLOPED OAK MOTH

LEOPARD MOTH

PARTHENICE TIGER MOTH

EMPEROR GUM MOTH

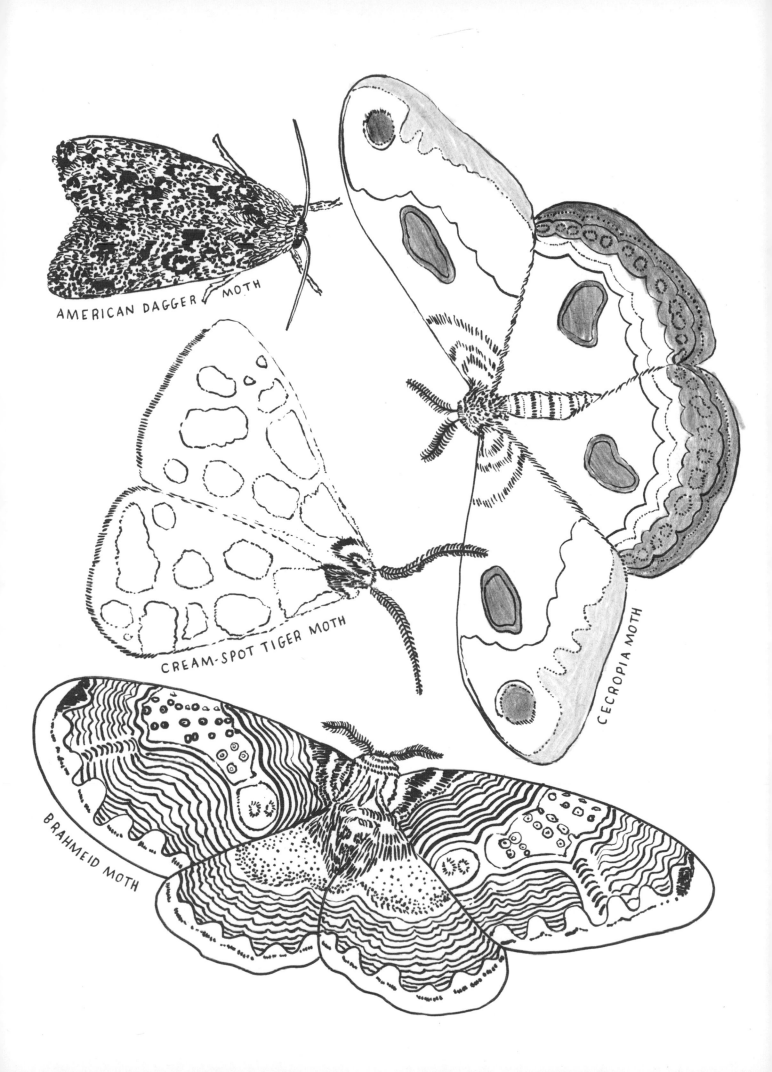

AMERICAN DAGGER MOTH

CREAM-SPOT TIGER MOTH

CECROPIA MOTH

BRAHMEID MOTH

FILL these PAGES WITH MANY MARVELOUS MOTHS and SPECTACULAR BUTTERFLIES

USE all YOUR MOST
COLORFUL PENS and PENCILS

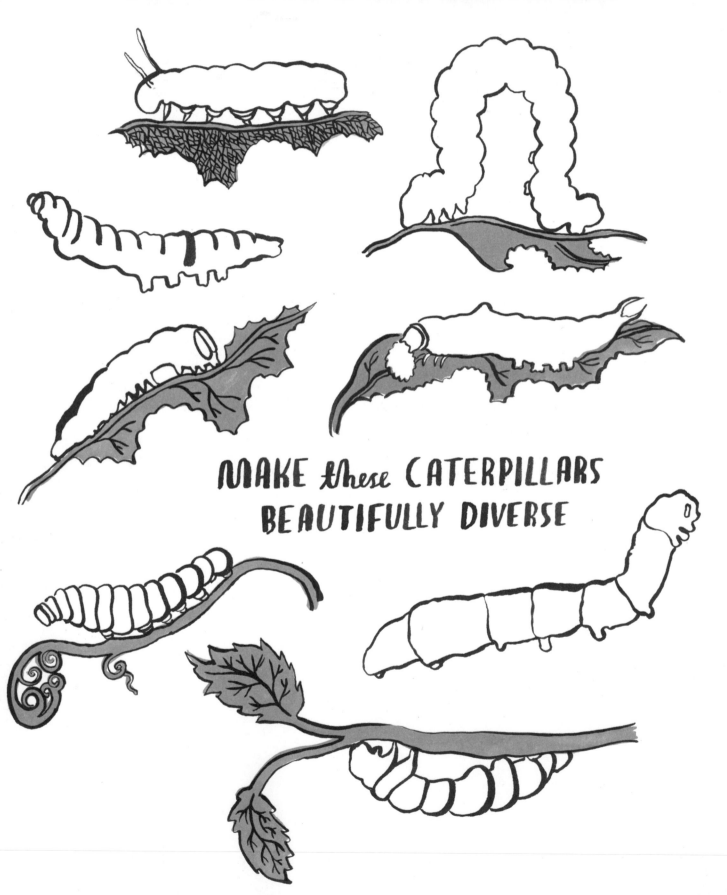

GIVE SOME SPOTS,
OTHERS STRIPES

SOME COULD have SPIKY SPINES,
OTHERS HAIRY LASHES

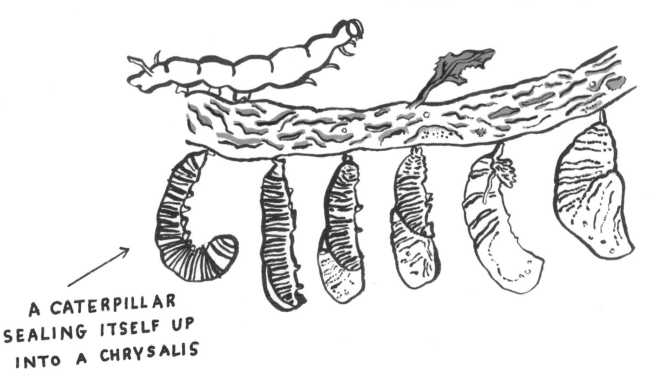

A CATERPILLAR
SEALING ITSELF UP
INTO A CHRYSALIS

CATERPILLARS LOVE TO EAT

SEE the HOLES in THE LEAVES
WHERE THE CATERPILLARS HAVE BEEN CHOMPING AWAY?

CATERPILLARS are MOSTLY HERBIVORES
WHICH MEANS THEY
LIKE EATING PLANTS

DRAW the MISSING
CATERPILLARS ON TO
THESE LEAVES

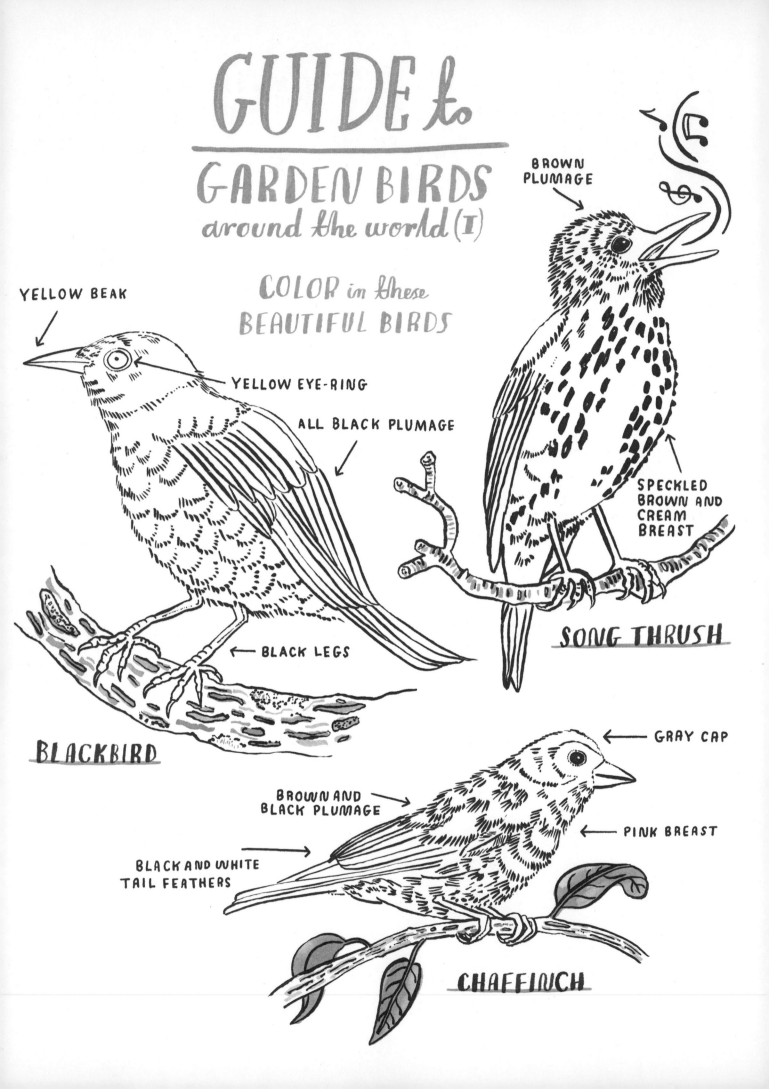

EARLY ONE SPRING MORNING OPEN YOUR BEDROOM WINDOW and JUST... LISTEN

CAN YOU HEAR any BIRDS...?

Look at me, Look at me, Look at me, do.

BIRD SONGS are OFTEN ABOUT WARNING OTHER MALES TO KEEP AWAY or TRYING TO WOO a FEMALE

WHAT do YOU THINK THESE BIRDS are SINGING ABOUT?

THREE CHEERS for SPRING !

Write a list of ALL the things you
LOVE about SPRING

Listen out for the ROBIN
singing loudly in spring

DRAW a robin on THIS PAGE

HOW to GROW SPROUT HEADS

YOU WILL NEED:
- SPROUT seeds
- YOGURT POTS
- COTTON BALLS
- MARKER PENS

① TAKE the LABEL OFF THE YOGURT POT

② GET your MARKER PENS and DRAW ON A FACE

③ WET the COTTON BALLS and PUT IN THE BOTTOM of THE YOGURT POT

④ DAMPEN SOME more COTTON BALLS and PUT IT ON TOP OF THE FIRST, LEAVING SOME SPACE at THE TOP OF THE POT

⑤ SPRINKLE SOME SPROUT SEEDS ON TO the COTTON BALLS

⑥ PUT the POT SOMEWHERE WARM and LIGHT... A SUNNY WINDOWSILL WOULD be PERFECT

⑦ REPEAT WITH the REST OF THE YOGURT POTS

⑧ AFTER about A WEEK YOUR SPROUT HEADS SHOULD have A FULL HEAD OF HAIR!

MAKE an EGG SALAD SANDWICH with SPROUTS

YUM... BEST SANDWICH EVER*

YOU WILL NEED:

- 2 LARGE EGGS
- Mayonnaise
- 4 SLICES of BREAD
- Butter
- SPROUTS

① Hard **BOIL** the EGGS and leave to COOL
WHEN cool, shell and RINSE the EGGS

② PUT the eggs in a MIXING BOWL and
MASH with a FORK

③ ADD a **FEW** spoons of MAYONNAISE,
several snips of SPROUTS,
A PINCH of SALT and pepper,
and MIX WELL

④ BUTTER the BREAD and FILL one
slice WITH a nice thick LAYER of EGG
MIXTURE, going right UP TO the CRUSTS.
TOP with a SECOND SLICE of BREAD
and PRESS down FIRMLY

*YOU MIGHT DISAGREE!
WHAT'S YOUR FAVORITE SANDWICH?

⑤ CUT in HALF and ENJOY!

FILL this PAGE
   with DRAWINGS
      of your GROWING sproutheads

INVENT your OWN sandwich using SPROUTS.
WRITE down the RECIPE
HERE

↓

Mangoes and Watermelons

Picnics

OUTDOOR SWIMS

TIDEPOOLING

Sandcastles

HELLO

HOT

SUNNY

Grass whistles

GREEN

LONG DAYS

Blue skies

FOREST WALKS

LADYBUGS

Dandelions

CAMPING

INSECTS

Daisy chains

SCRAPBOOKS

SUMMER

Walking barefoot

ROSE PETAL PERFUME

DANCING DRAGONFLIES

Raspberries and Strawberries

Leaves and Flowers

ANATOMY
of a leaf

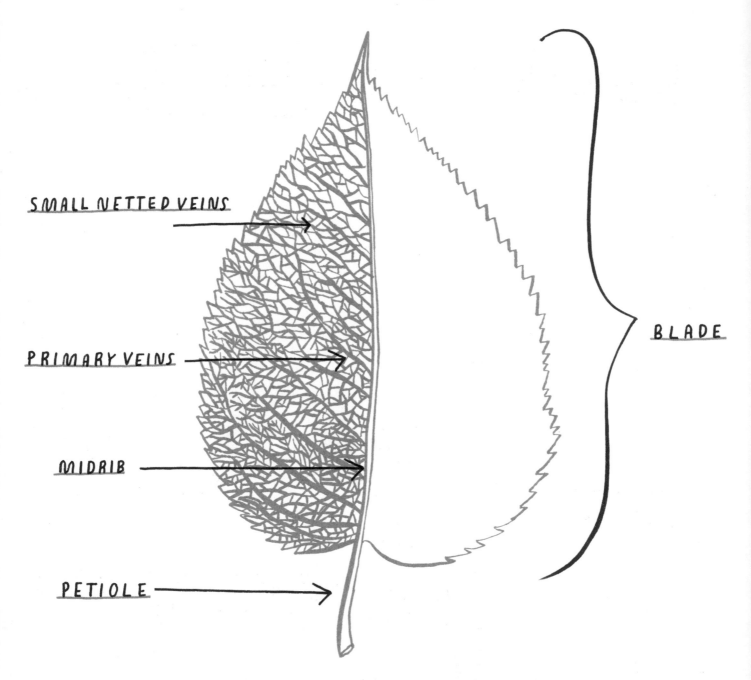

SMALL NETTED VEINS

PRIMARY VEINS

MIDRIB

PETIOLE

BLADE

Draw in the missing veins
on the right-hand side of the leaf

Draw lots of veins on to this leaf

The leaf is the most wonderful factory on earth

The more veins a leaf has, the faster it can convert sunshine into food

SILVER MAPLE

Draw the MIDRIB and VEINS
on to these OAK LEAVES

CHESTNUT OAK

BLACKJACK OAK

ENGLISH OAK

SPANISH OAK

PYRENEAN OAK

ALGERIAN OAK

HUNGARIAN OAK

MOSSY CUP OAK

CHAMPION OAK

SCARLET OAK

PIN OAK

CALIFORNIAN
BLACK OAK

WHITE OAK

JAPANESE BLUE OAK

SESSILE OAK

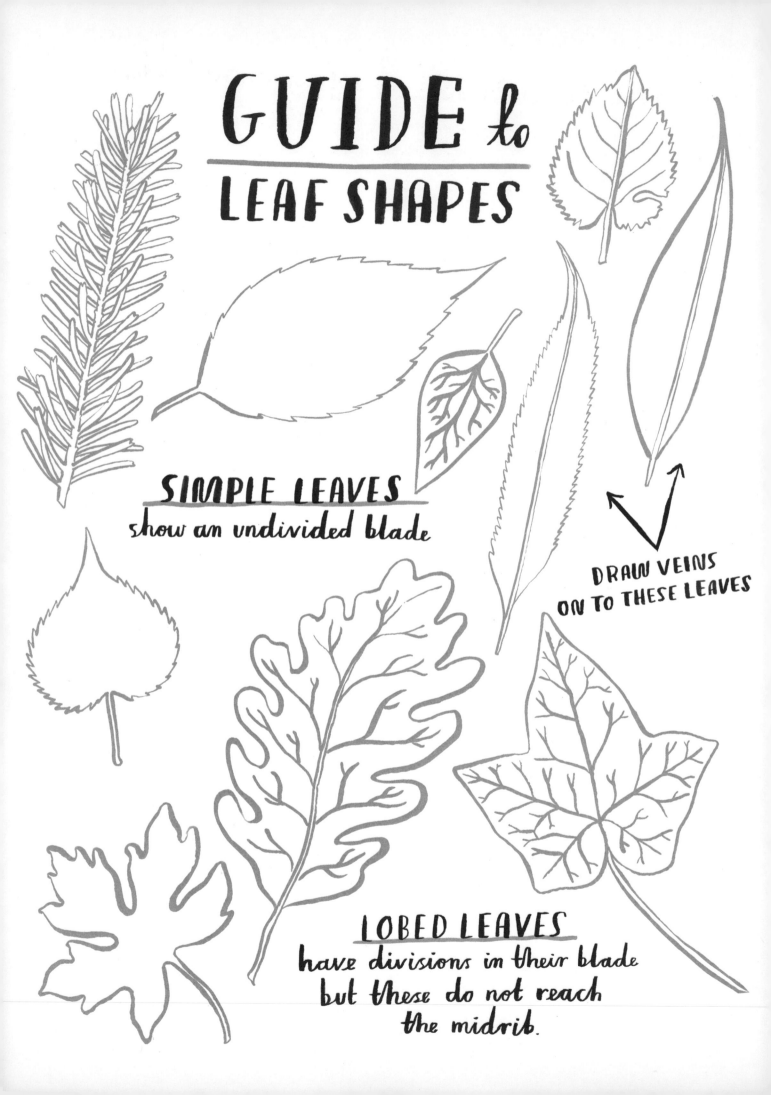

GUIDE to LEAF SHAPES

SIMPLE LEAVES
show an undivided blade

DRAW VEINS
ON TO THESE LEAVES

LOBED LEAVES
have divisions in their blade
but these do not reach
the midrib.

COMPOUND LEAVES have a fragmented blade,

with divisions reaching the midrib.
Sometimes each one of these fragments
is similar to a single leaf.
They are called **LEAFLETS**.

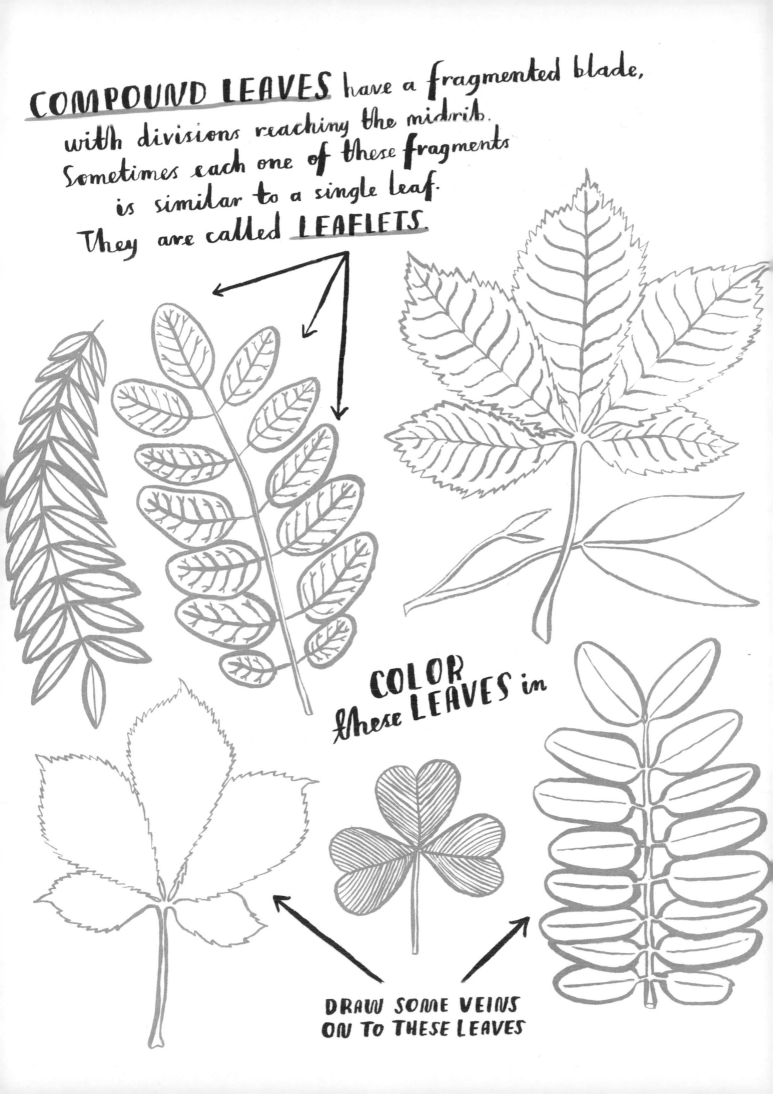

COLOR
these LEAVES in

DRAW SOME VEINS
ON TO THESE LEAVES

① COLLECT a SELECTION of fallen
Leaves from the SIDEWALK,
the PARK or your GARDEN

② Separate them into PILES of
SIMPLE, LOBED, and
COMPOUND LEAVES

DRAW your
SIMPLE and LOBED LEAVES
on this page

Draw your
COMPOUND LEAVES
on this page

DRAW wide-reaching ROOTS FOR this OAK TREE

DRAW your FAVORITE TREE on THIS page

DRAW the REST OF THE TREE

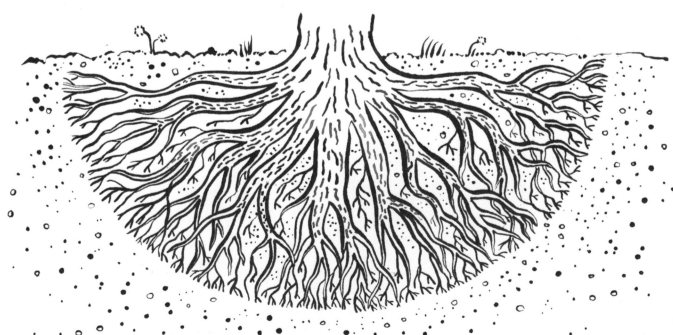

A TREE GETS MOISTURE and NUTRIENTS
FROM THE SOIL THROUGH ITS ROOTS

DO YOU KNOW WHICH TREES these LEAVES COME FROM ?

\- \- \- \- \- \- \-

\- \- \- \- \- \-

\- \- \- \- \-

\- \- \- \- \- \-

\- \- \- \- \-

\- \- \- \- \- \-

THE ANSWERS ARE SOMEWHERE IN THIS BOOK. CAN YOU FIND THEM?

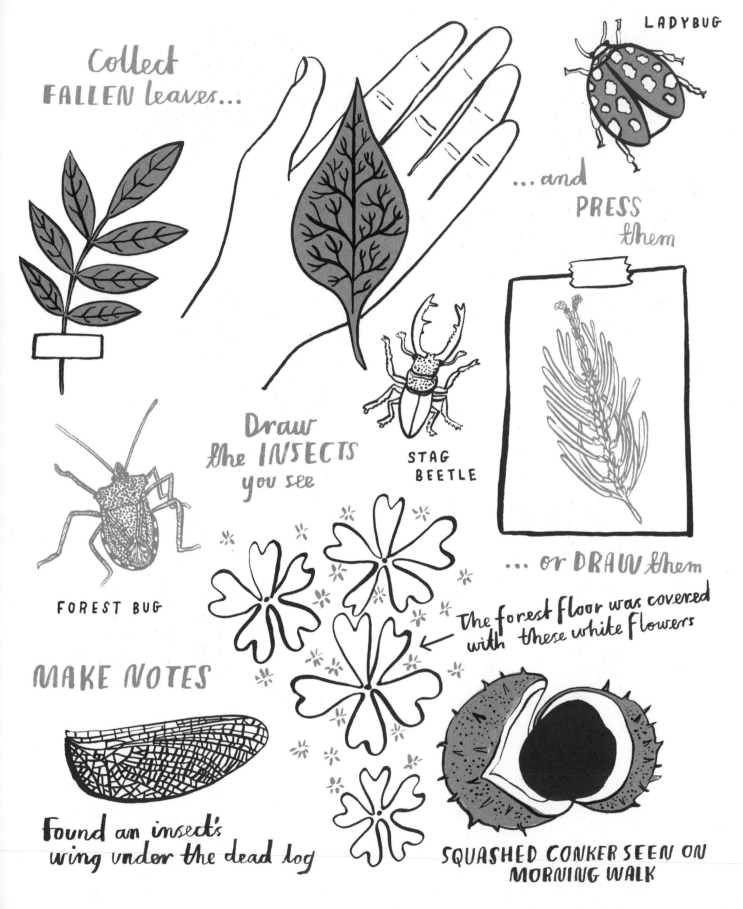

NOTE DOWN the SMELLS of THE FOREST

...DAMP?
... WOODY?
...EARTHY?

IF YOU are in a PINE FOREST, collect some FALLEN pine cones to DRAW Later on

LOOK OUT FOR TRACKS

Hello beautiful owl

SAW this PAW PRINT today... BADGER?

FOUND an interesting MUSHROOM to DRAW

ONE HALF OF A HELICOPTER SEED

LOOK UP!

What do you see?

CREATE INTRICATE PATTERNS FOR these BEETLES

ANATOMY
of a beetle

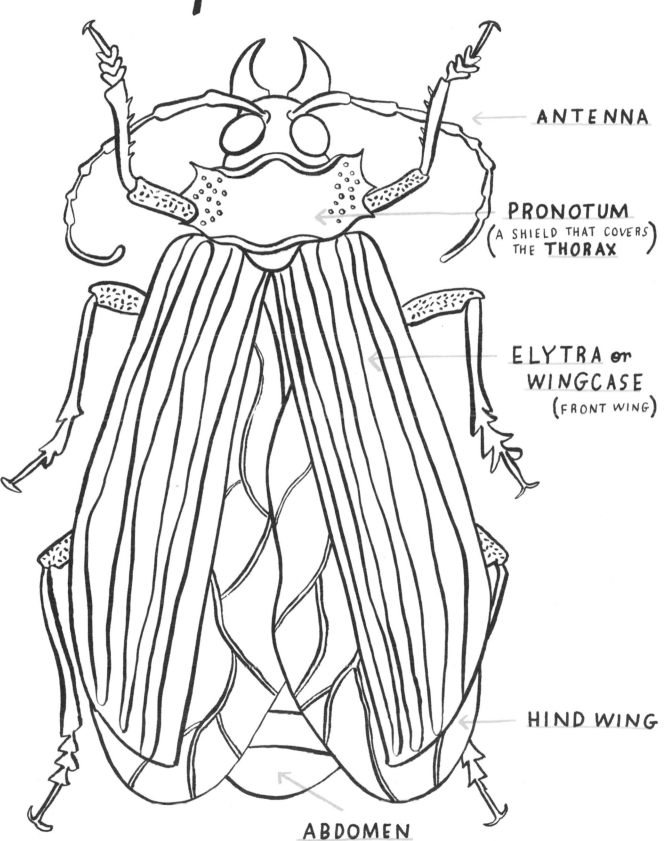

ANTENNA

PRONOTUM
(A SHIELD THAT COVERS)
THE THORAX

ELYTRA or
WINGCASE
(FRONT WING)

HIND WING

ABDOMEN

FILL these PAGES with DRAWINGS of BEETLES

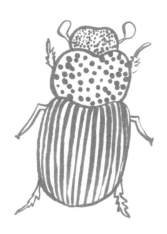

BEETLES are THE LARGEST GROUP of living organisms ON OUR PLANET

LOTS and LOTS OF THEM
Large and SMALL, and WITH
THE colors OF PRECIOUS GEMS

There ARE at least -350,000- SPECIES,
and THERE may BE MANY more yet
TO be DISCOVERED

ANATOMY
of a tree

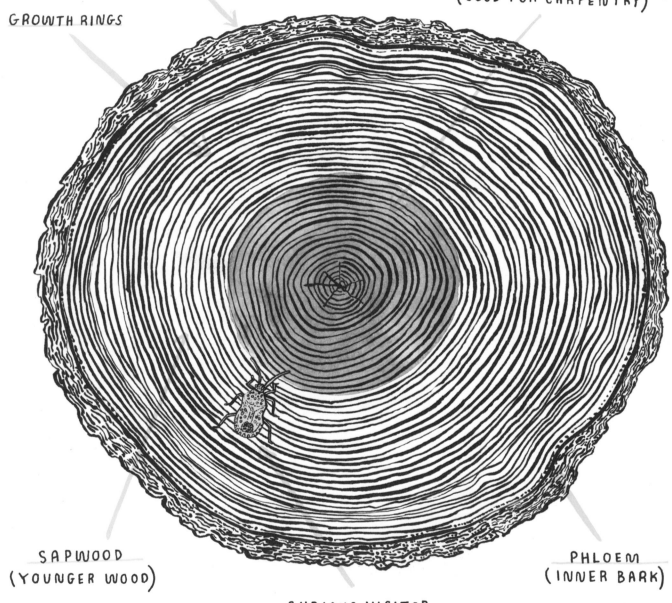

OUTER BARK

GROWTH RINGS

HEARTWOOD
(GOOD FOR CARPENTRY)

SAPWOOD
(YOUNGER WOOD)

PHLOEM
(INNER BARK)

CURIOUS VISITOR

If YOU sliced THROUGH a TREE TRUNK what WOULD YOU see?

DRAW GROWTH RINGS
ON TO this TREE TRUNK

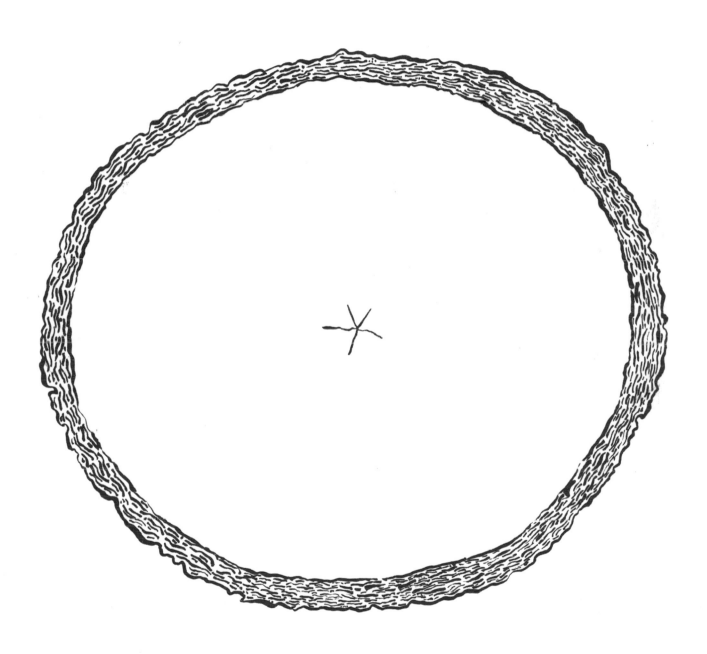

Each RING represents A YEAR of GROWTH
HOW old WILL YOUR TREE be?

Have YOU NOTICED how TREE BARK comes IN DIFFERENT and WONDERFUL PATTERNS?

Make A RUBBING by CUTTING OUT this PAGE, HOLDING it UP against A TREE and COVERING the PAGE using OIL PASTELS or CHARCOAL

MAKE another TREE BARK RUBBING ON this PAGE

BY THE SEA

MAKE SAILING VESSELS OUT OF LEAVES, TWIGS, SHELLS, and DRIFTWOOD

IF YOU MAKE A FEW YOU CAN HAVE a RACE WITH THEM

YOU are AT THE BEACH

What's on your horizon...?

_____

YOU are AT THE BEACH

What's on your horizon...?

DRAW what YOU SEE

GUIDE to SHELLS

AND *the* CREATURES THAT LIVE IN THEM

CHITONS

MARINE MOLLUSCS THAT
LIVE MOSTLY ON ROCKS

BIVALVES

MOLLUSCS THAT LIVE IN
TWO EQUALLY SIZED SHELLS
JOINED BY A HINGE

CEPHALOPODS

HAVE TENTACLES AND LIKE
LIVING IN SALT WATER

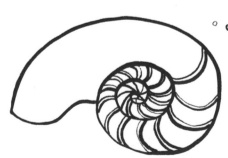

CROSS-SECTION OF
NAUTILUS POMPILIUS

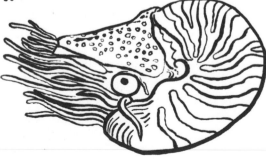

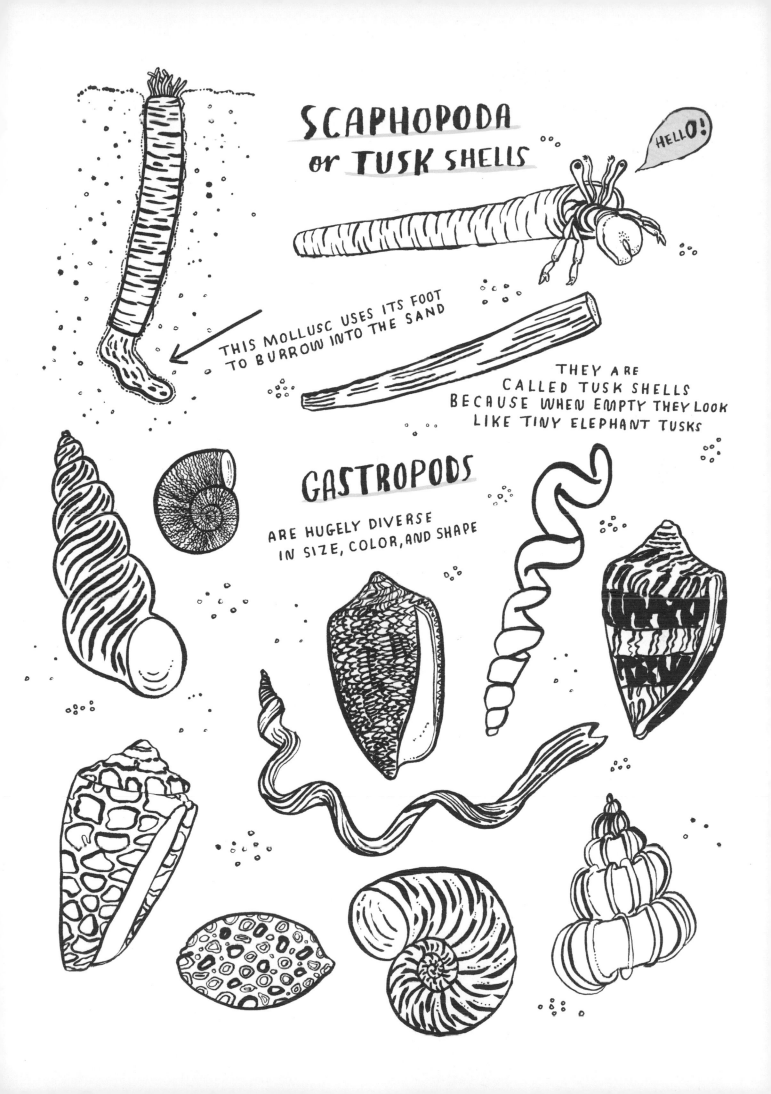

ON THE BEACH

COLLECT EMPTY SHELLS that YOU LIKE AND DRAW them HERE...

...CAN YOU IDENTIFY WHICH groups THE SHELLS BELONG TO ?...

ON THE BEACH

SEAWEED COMES IN LOTS OF WONDERFUL SHAPES, SIZES, and COLORS

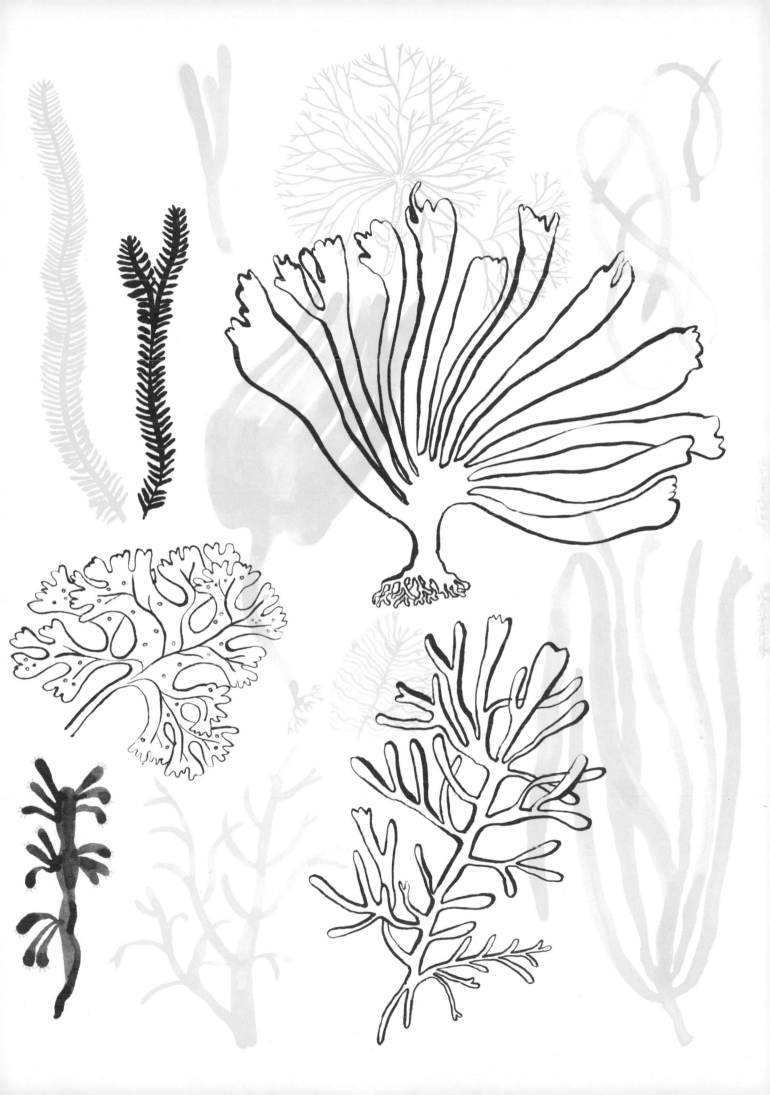

SEE any INTERESTING SEAWEED ON THE BEACH ?
DRAW them ON THESE PAGES

PAINT on to STONES

I like using WHITE paint on DARK stones

Choose SMOOTH stones
and WASH and DRY them
before PAINTING

Practice YOUR designs on any
BLANK stones THAT YOU see here

Ideas for stones: FISH, a leaf,
a FANTASTIC pattern, A COBWEB,
or ANYTHING you like

DECORATE *these* STONES

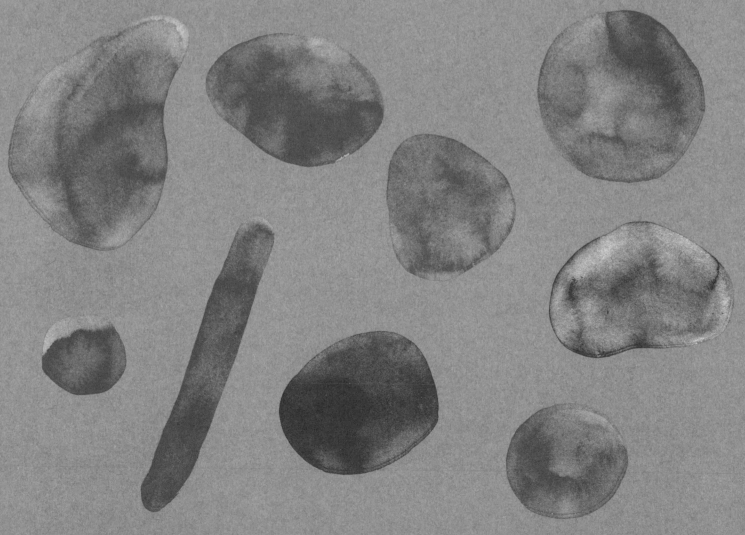

CREATE a PATTERN with PEBBLES

Fill these PAGES with PATTERNS YOU have NOTICED in NATURE

It could be the STRIPES on a BEETLE

It could be
the SPOTS
ON a FISH

HOW to GROW an AVOCADO TREE

EVER eaten an AVOCADO and looked at
THE big OLD PIT LEFT BEHIND?
Don't THROW it AWAY... PLANT IT!

① Wash the AVOCADO PIT and
let it DRY for 24 HOURS.

② CAREFULLY push 4 TOOTHPICKS
into THE thickest PART
of the AVOCADO PIT.

③ Fill A GLASS with WATER and SUSPEND
the PIT OVER it SO THAT the
ROUND PART is IN FRESH air AND
THE flat PART is SUBMERGED
in THE WATER.

④ Place THE GLASS on a SUNNY windowsill.

⑤ NOW you HAVE to WAIT... and THEN wait SOME MORE.
It can TAKE 3 to 6 WEEKS, sometimes LONGER.
Ponder THE PHILOSOPHER ARISTOTLE'S   WORDS
WHILST you WAIT:

PATIENCE IS BITTER,
BUT ITS
FRUIT IS SWEET.

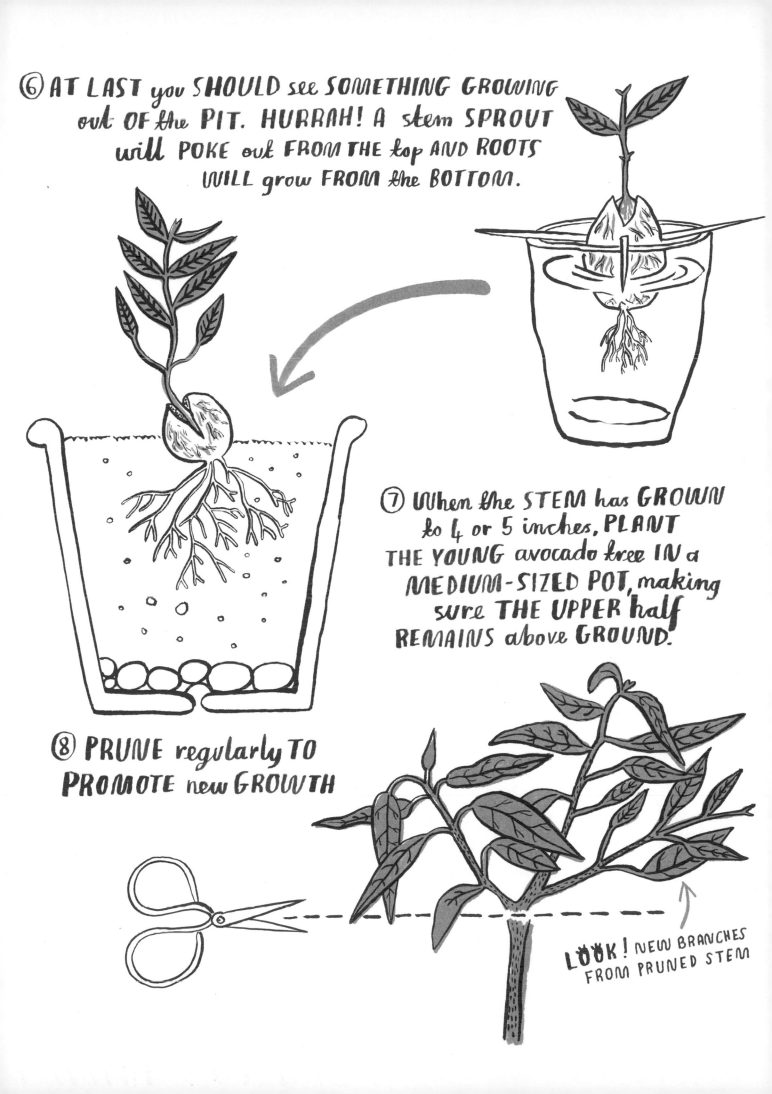

⑥ AT LAST you SHOULD see SOMETHING GROWING out OF the PIT. HURRAH! A stem SPROUT will POKE out FROM THE top AND ROOTS WILL grow FROM the BOTTOM.

⑦ When the STEM has GROWN to 4 or 5 inches, PLANT THE YOUNG avocado tree IN a MEDIUM-SIZED POT, making sure THE UPPER half REMAINS above GROUND.

⑧ PRUNE regularly TO PROMOTE new GROWTH

LOOK! NEW BRANCHES FROM PRUNED STEM

GUIDE to
GARDEN BIRDS
around the world (II)

GOLDEN ORIOLE

BLACK MARKING AROUND EYE

RAINBOW LORIKEET

BLUE HEAD

RED BEAK

RED RIM AROUND BLACK EYE

YELLOW NECK

BLACK WINGS

YELLOW BODY

RED BREAST

YELLOW AND GREEN PLUMAGE

BLUE CAP

PALE BLUE BACK

BLUE AND BLACK WINGS

LIGHT GRAY BREAST

BLUEJAY

GREEN WINGS

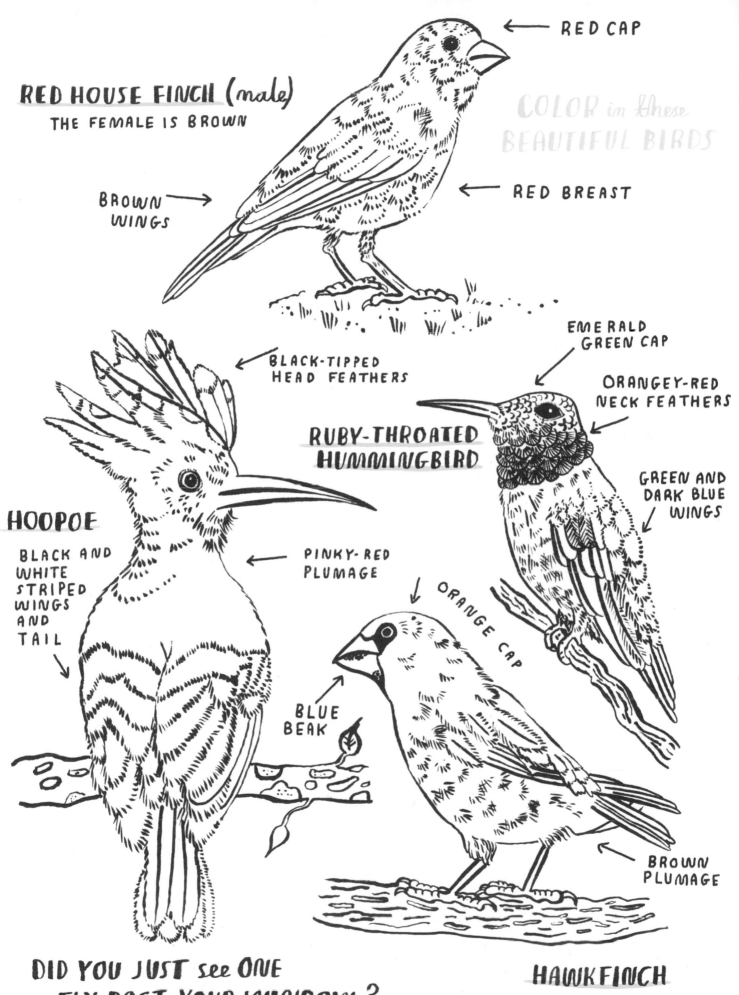

RED CAP

RED HOUSE FINCH (male)
THE FEMALE IS BROWN

COLOR in these
BEAUTIFUL BIRDS

BROWN WINGS

RED BREAST

EMERALD GREEN CAP

BLACK-TIPPED HEAD FEATHERS

ORANGEY-RED NECK FEATHERS

RUBY-THROATED HUMMINGBIRD

GREEN AND DARK BLUE WINGS

HOOPOE

BLACK AND WHITE STRIPED WINGS AND TAIL

PINKY-RED PLUMAGE

ORANGE CAP

BLUE BEAK

BROWN PLUMAGE

DID YOU JUST see ONE FLY PAST YOUR WINDOW?

HAWKFINCH

DRAW lots OF LITTLE BIRDS on this page

Ruby

Herbert

Jack

Hariet

Jenny

CAN you SEE ANY BIRDS
OUT of YOUR WINDOW?

These PAGES are FOR
YOUR drawings OF BIRDS

DRAW lots OF BIRDS on THESE PAGES

Why NOT DRAW them FLYING in THE SKY?

If YOU see A FEATHER ON the GROUND PICK it UP AND start A FEATHER COLLECTION

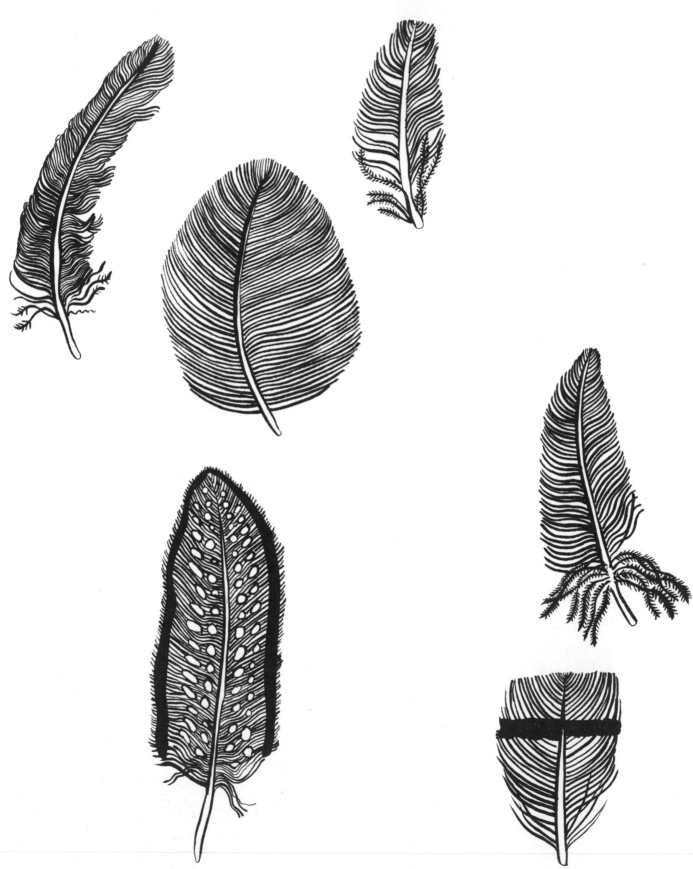

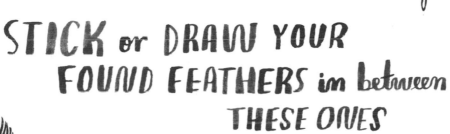
STICK or DRAW YOUR
FOUND FEATHERS in between
THESE ONES

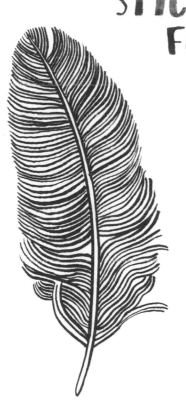

ANATOMY
of a feather

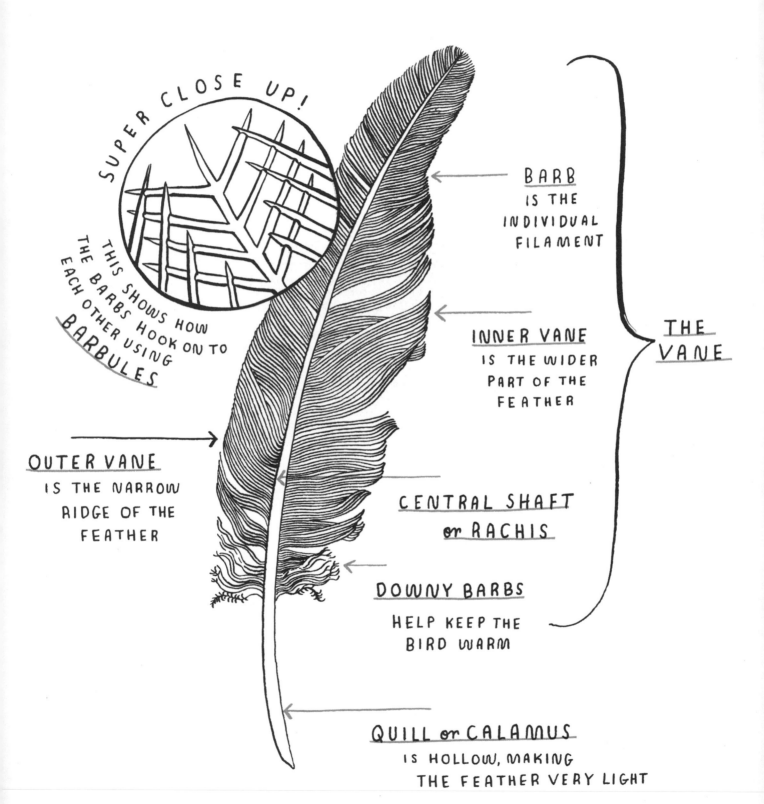

SUPER CLOSE UP!

THIS SHOWS HOW THE BARBS HOOK ON TO EACH OTHER USING BARBULES

BARB
IS THE INDIVIDUAL FILAMENT

INNER VANE
IS THE WIDER PART OF THE FEATHER

THE VANE

OUTER VANE
IS THE NARROW RIDGE OF THE FEATHER

CENTRAL SHAFT or RACHIS

DOWNY BARBS
HELP KEEP THE BIRD WARM

QUILL or CALAMUS
IS HOLLOW, MAKING THE FEATHER VERY LIGHT

If YOU come ACROSS a FEATHER on YOUR WALK, WHY not STICK it HERE?

DRAW birds SITTING on the TELEPHONE POLE wires

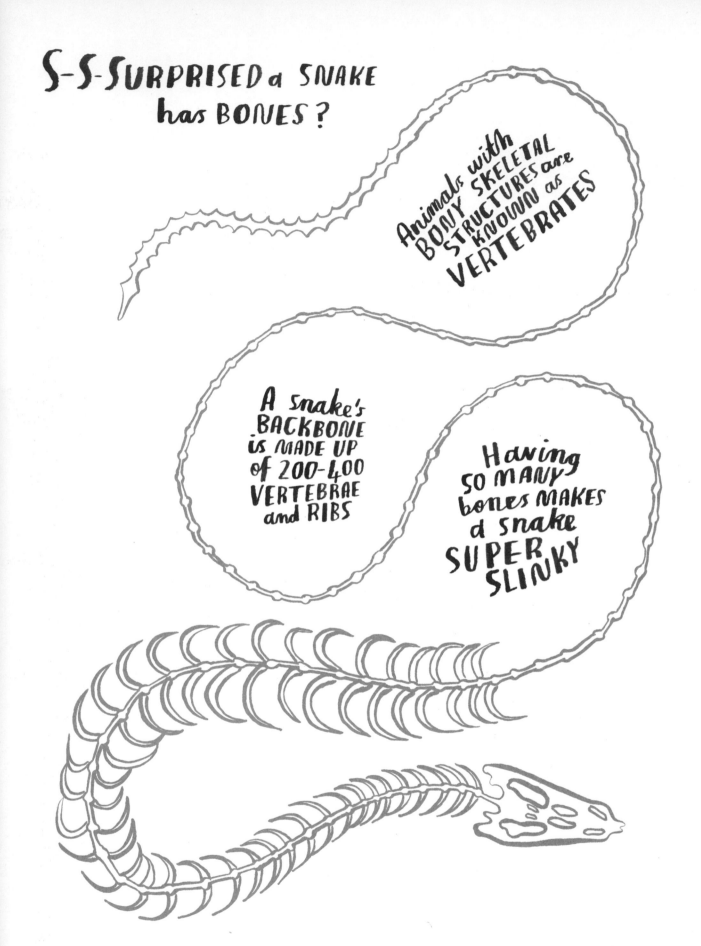

There are ABOUT 3000 species of snake in THE WORLD

DRAW scales ON to THIS snake

Snakes SMELL with their TONGUES

SNIFF

SNIFF

FILL these PAGES
with patterns YOU have
NOTICED in NATURE

IT
COULD
be a
cluster
OF
pine cone
SCALES

It could be within THE within scales of a snake

GUIDE to
DAISIES

Shasta Daisy

African Daisy

Livingstone Daisy

Barberton Daisy

Ox-eye Daisy

Gerbera Daisy

Michaelmas Daisy

Gloriosa Daisy

COLOR these IN
PICK YOUR FAVORITE

Prairie Daisy

Tahoka Daisy

Marguerite Daisy

Black-Eyed Susan

Cowpen Daisy

Lazy Daisy

Kingfisher Daisy

Zulu Prince Daisy

Butter Daisy

FILL these PAGES
with all KINDS of DAISIES

HOW to MAKE a DAISY CHAIN

YOU WILL NEED:

- Lots of DAISIES
- NIMBLE FINGERS

① Pinch INTO the BOTTOM of the DAISY STALK using your THUMBNAIL

② Keep pressing UNTIL a small SLIT forms →

③ CAREFULLY thread another DAISY STEM through the SLIT and PULL THE head taut AGAINST it

④ Keep going UNTIL YOU'VE used up all your daisies

⑤ JOIN UP your first and YOUR last DAISY AND there you HAVE it .....

A beautiful DAISY CHAIN!

Wear it LIKE a CROWN
Wear it ROUND YOUR NECK

Wear it ANY WAY YOU LIKE!

THE DANDELION FLOWER USES WIND to DISPERSE its DELICATE SEEDS

DRAW the GENTLE DANDELION SEEDS DRIFTING ACROSS the PAGES

SUMMER IS THE TIME FOR FLOWERS
You see them blooming everywhere

on THIS PAGE
DRAW YOUR FAVORITE
SUMMERTIME FLOWER

LONG LIVE SUMMER!
WRITE a LIST OF ALL THE THINGS YOU LOVE ABOUT SUMMER

YOU WILL NEED:
- Your THUMBS
- A BLADE of GRASS

① Hold the BLADE of GRASS taut between the top and BOTTOM of your thumbs

② Blow hard INTO the SPACE BETWEEN your THUMBS, vibrating the BLADE of GRASS and CREATING a whistling sound

If it doesn't work, DON'T WORRY... keep practicing!

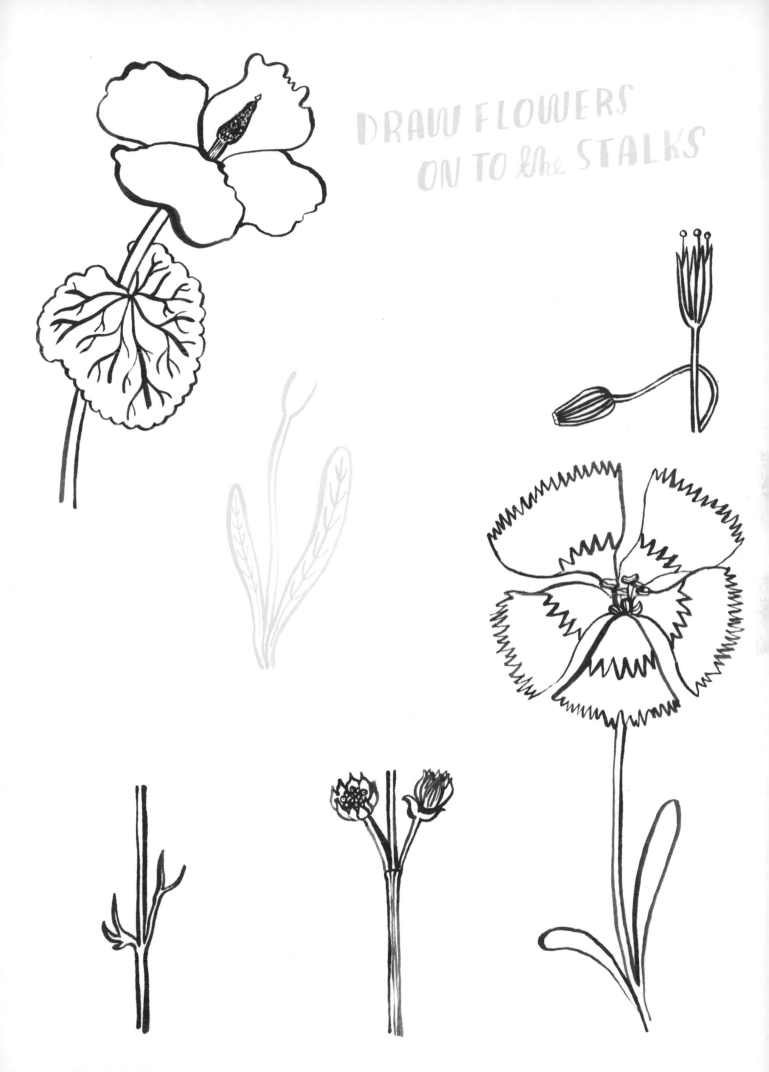

DRAW FLOWERS
ON TO the STALKS

DRAW·MORE· FLOWERS

Fill these PAGES
with PATTERNS YOU have
NOTICED in NATURE

It
could
be the
DASHES
on
a
bird
feather

It
could be
dots ON
THE wings
of a moth

WONDERFUL, HARD-WORKING, CLEVER BEES

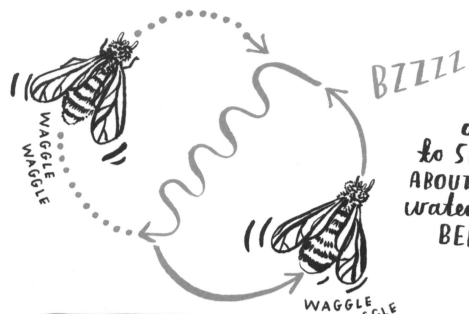

WAGGLE WAGGLE

BZZZZ

WAGGLE WAGGLE

Bees do a WAGGLE DANCE to SHARE information ABOUT NEARBY flowers, watering HOLES, or new BEEHIVE LOCATIONS

Bees have discovered THAT the HEXAGON is THE best, MOST efficient SHAPE to USE WHEN they make THE cells in THEIR HIVE. It helps SUPPORT all THE other cells, uses the LEAST amount of BEESWAX and PROVIDES the MAXIMUM storage space for HONEY.

The flower GIVES the BEE NECTAR in EXCHANGE for POLLEN

The Pollen sticks to the bee's legs and body

BZZZZ

BZZZZ

The BEE carries the DUSTY to other FLOWERS HELPING to MAKE POLLEN off nearby, NEW PLANTS

CREATORS of HONEY and POLLINATORS of MOST OF the WORLD'S CROPS

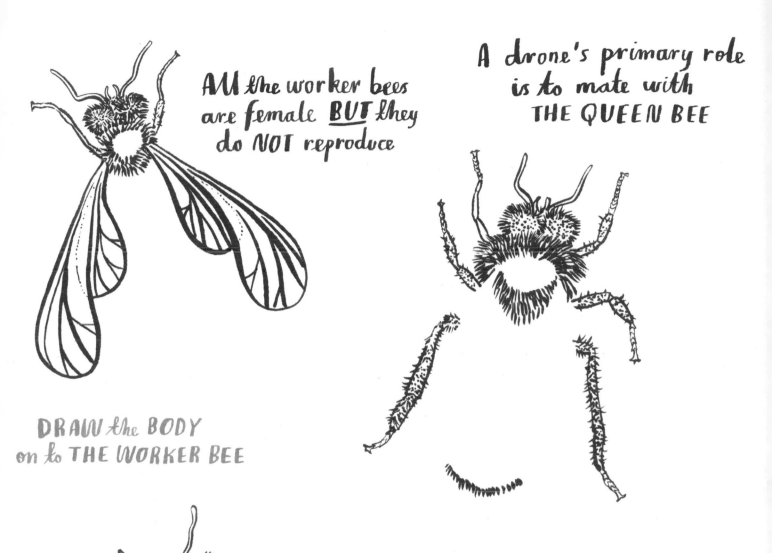

All the worker bees are female **BUT** they do **NOT** reproduce

A drone's primary role is to mate with THE QUEEN BEE

DRAW the BODY on to THE WORKER BEE

DRAW the WINGS on to THE DRONE BEE

There is only one QUEEN and she is the MOTHER of ALL the BEES in the hive

DRAW the LEGS on to THE QUEEN BEE

PAINT the ROSES DIFFERENT COLORS
as BEES ARE ATTRACTED TO
CONTRASTING FLOWERS

HOW to MAKE ROSE PETAL PERFUME

YOU WILL NEED:
- 2 CUPS of ROSE PETALS
- 2 Bowls
- Pestle and mortar OR spoon
- SIEVE
- A JAR to PUT your perfume in

① Place the ROSE PETALS in A BOWL. POUR some WARM WATER over the PETALS making sure they are all covered. LEAVE to SOAK for an hour.

② AFTER an hour, lift out the ROSE PETALS carefully, LEAVING BEHIND the WATER in the bowl.

③ Mash the PETALS in another bowl USING the back of a spoon OR a PESTLE and MORTAR if you have one. THIS HELPS the petals release their WONDERFUL aroma.

④ PUT the ROSE PETALS back in THE bowl of WATER and LEAVE for a further 2 to 3 HOURS.

⑤ After the petals HAVE had a GOOD long soak, STRAIN the MIXTURE through a SIEVE.

⑥ Pour the PRECIOUS ELIXIR into a jar and your PERFUME is ready to use!

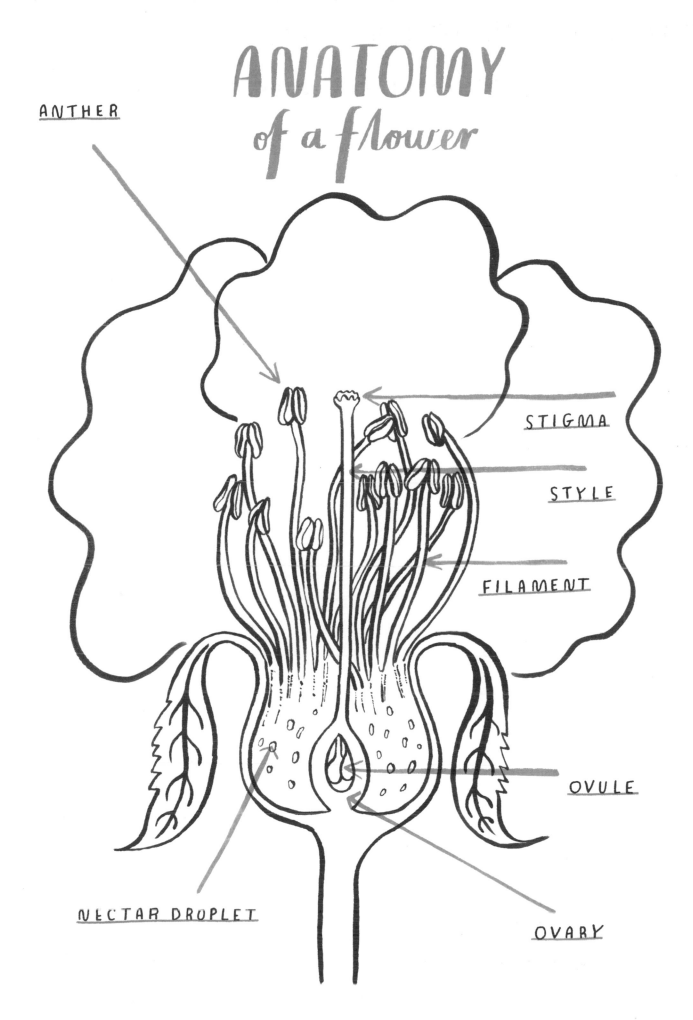

ANATOMY
of a flower

ANTHER

STIGMA

STYLE

FILAMENT

NECTAR DROPLET

OVULE

OVARY

YOU are LYING IN THE GRASS
What's on your horizon...?

DRAW what YOU SEE

There are thought to be 200 MILLION insects for EVERY human on the planet

Do YOU have a favorite insect?
MAYBE it's a BEE, an ANT, or an EARWIG?

Draw your FAVORITE insect
ON this PAGE

Write DOWN EVERYTHING
you know ABOUT YOUR favorite insect

WHERE does it live?

HOW LONG does it live?

ANY OTHER interesting info?

Draw the SNAILS coming out
from UNDERNEATH their shells

Well HELLO, wee beasties...

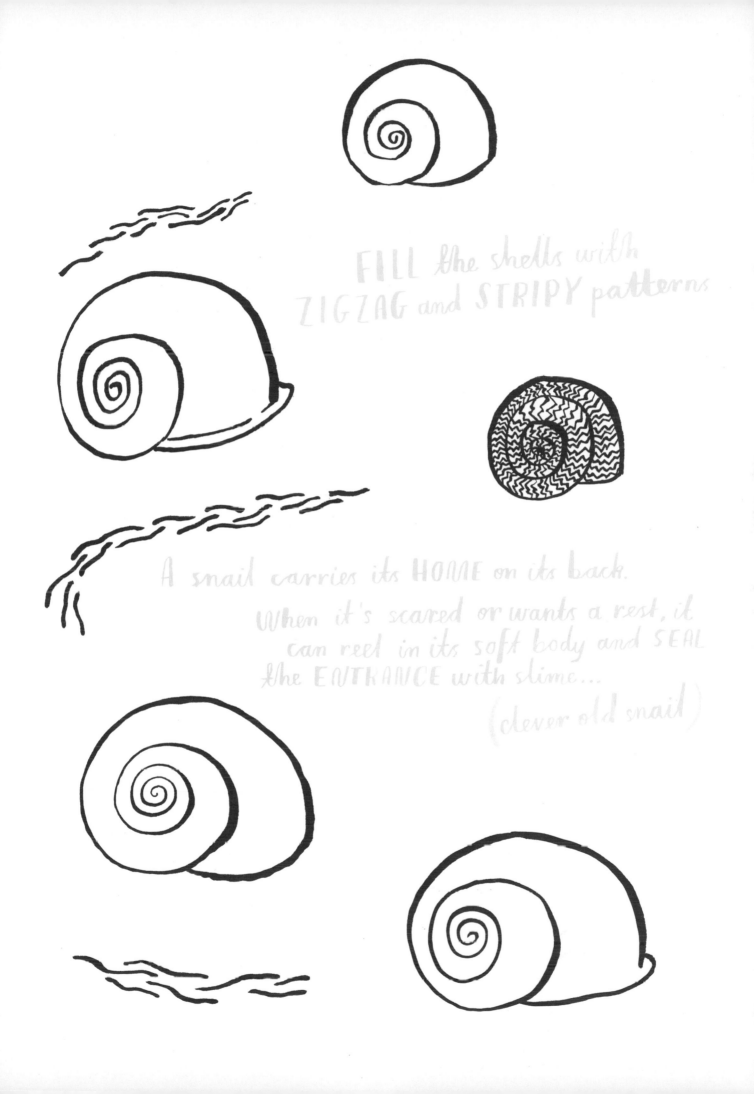

FILL the shells with
ZIGZAG and STRIPY patterns

A snail carries its HOME on its back.

When it's scared or wants a rest, it
can reel in its soft body and SEAL
the ENTRANCE with slime...

(clever old snail)

Snails and slugs make SLIME
   from special GLANDS which helps them
to GLIDE along the GROUND and
       protect them from sharp objects

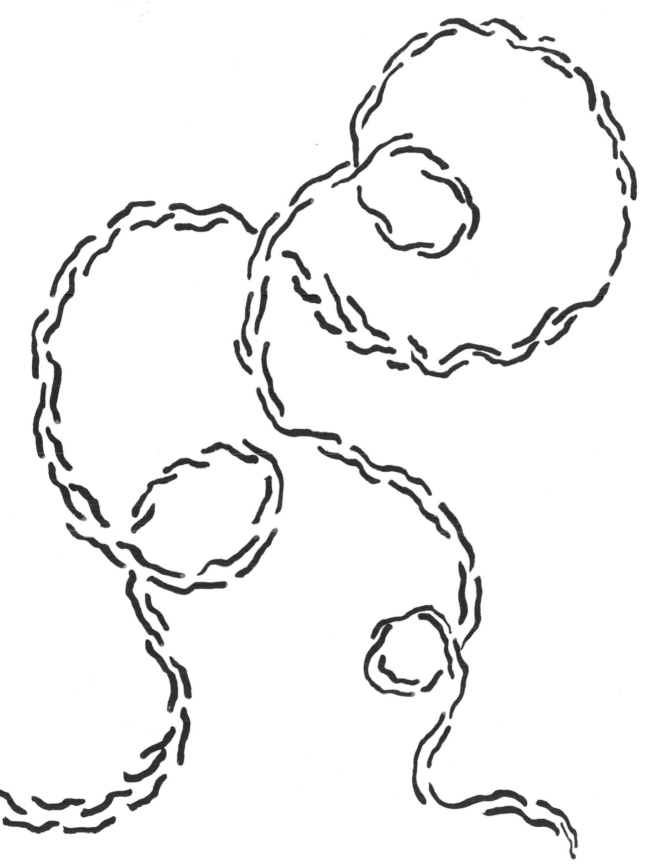

DRAW the SNAIL
at the end of this trail

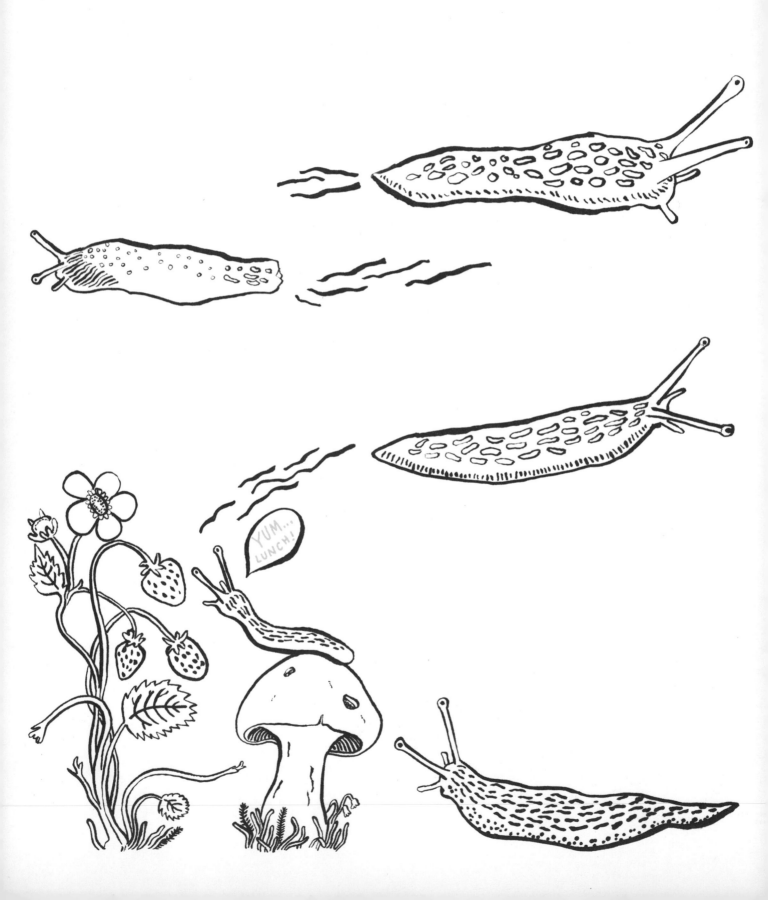

Draw shells on to
THESE SLUGS and
TURN them into SNAILS

Draw the PLANTS growing from these ROOTS

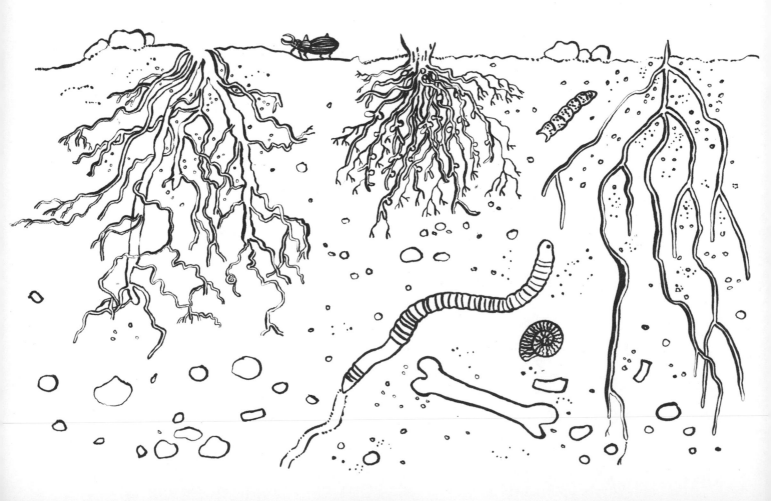

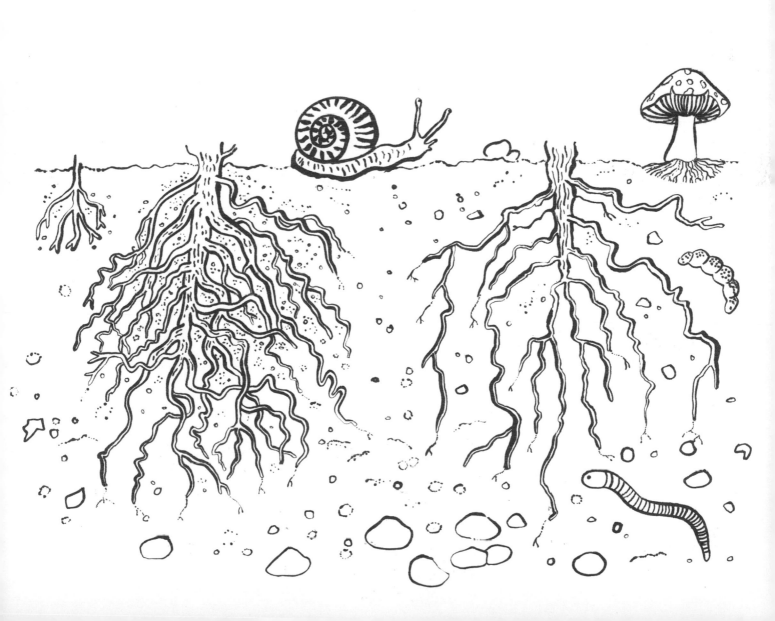

FOXES, moles, CHIPMUNKS, badgers, OTTERS, SHREWS, and EARTHWORMS all make their homes UNDERGROUND

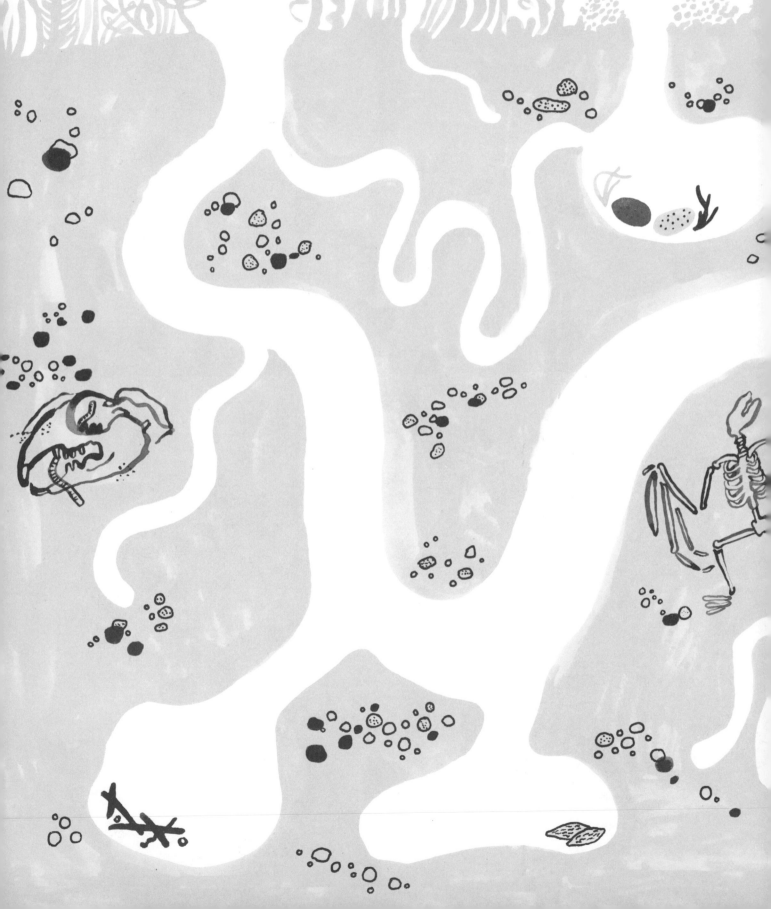

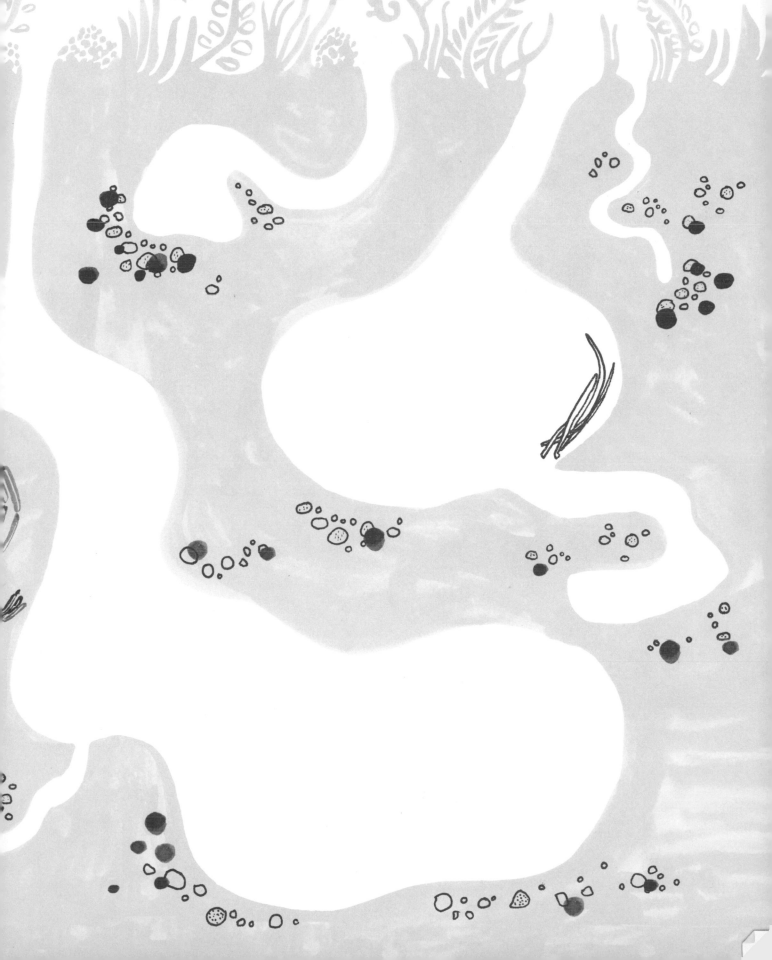

Draw SOME CREATURES that
MIGHT live in THESE BURROWS

SENSITIVE FERN

BRISTLE FERN

Fern leaves are called FRONDS

The FANTASTIC FERN

HAIRY LIP FERN

SEA SPLEENWORT

ROCK CAP FERN

They were among the FIRST plants on earth

ROYAL FERN

CLIMBING FERN

FRAGRANT FERN

There are about 12,000 different species of FERN worldwide

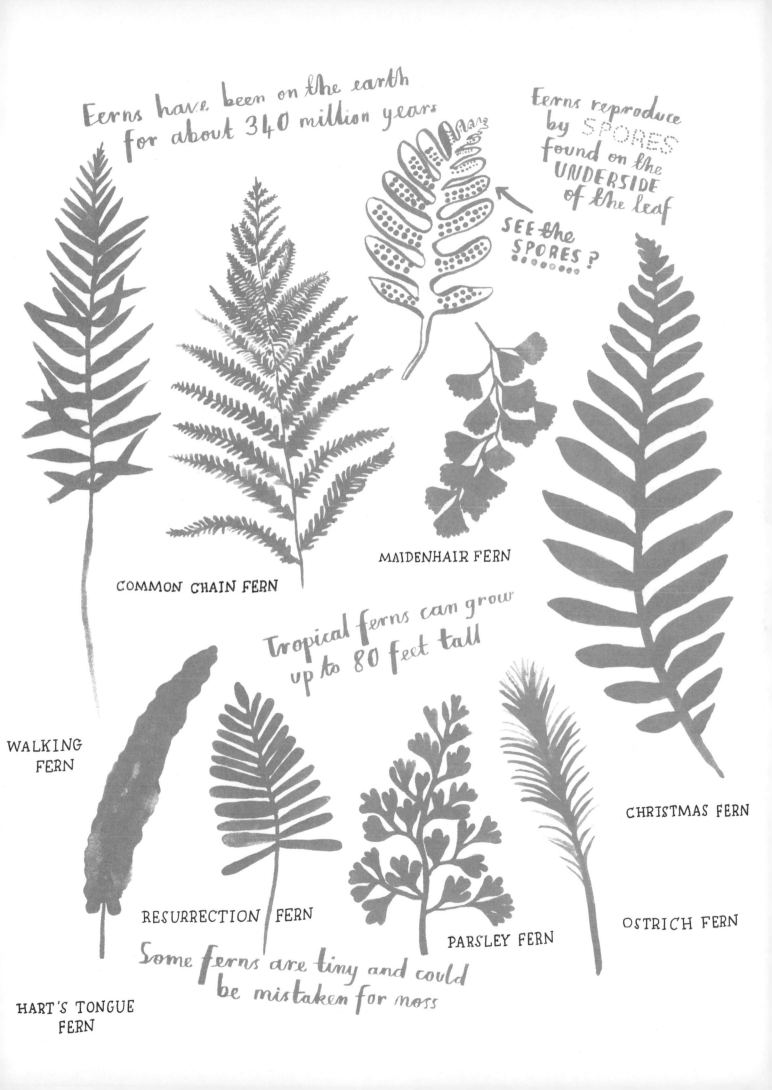

Ferns have been on the earth for about 340 million years

Ferns reproduce by SPORES found on the UNDERSIDE of the leaf

SEE the SPORES?

COMMON CHAIN FERN

MAIDENHAIR FERN

Tropical ferns can grow up to 80 feet tall

WALKING FERN

CHRISTMAS FERN

RESURRECTION FERN

PARSLEY FERN

OSTRICH FERN

Some ferns are tiny and could be mistaken for moss

HART'S TONGUE FERN

Fill these PAGES with drawings of your FAVORITE ferns

THEY are SUCH FUN TO DRAW

GROW a MINI FERNARIUM

YOU WILL NEED:

- Compost OR soil
- Small ferns
- Glass jar OR bottle with a lid
- small stones

① ARRANGE the small stones so that they COVER the BOTTOM of the GLASS JAR or BOTTLE. This creates a DRAINAGE layer.

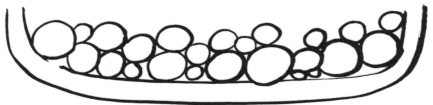

✳ LIKE MOST PLANTS, the FERN DOESN'T LIKE ITS ROOTS TO SIT in WATER.

② COVER the stones with COMPOST or SOIL.

③ Carefully place your FERNS into the glass bottle and GENTLY push the roots into the soil.

④ SPRINKLE a little water on to your FERNS and put the lid on to TRAP moisture.

⑤ Place your FERNARIUM in a shady spot.

HAVE FUN WATCHING YOUR FERNS GROW

CHESTNUTS

CRISPY

ACORNS

CRACKLING

BONFIRES

Building Burrows

HELLO

GOLD

Rainy

COOLER WEATHER

Snails and slugs

MAPLE TREES

Woodsmoke

Raking Leaves

BROWNS, ORANGES, and REDS

PUMPKINS

MISTY and FOGGY

Falling Leaves

Apples

FALL

Amber

Gusty

HARVESTING

Woodland Walks

LEAF PRINTS

MUSHROOM SEASON

NUT HUNT

The FASCINATING WORLD of FUNGI

Life on EARTH exists in FIVE KINGDOMS

Animalia

Plantae

FUNGI

Protista

Bacteria

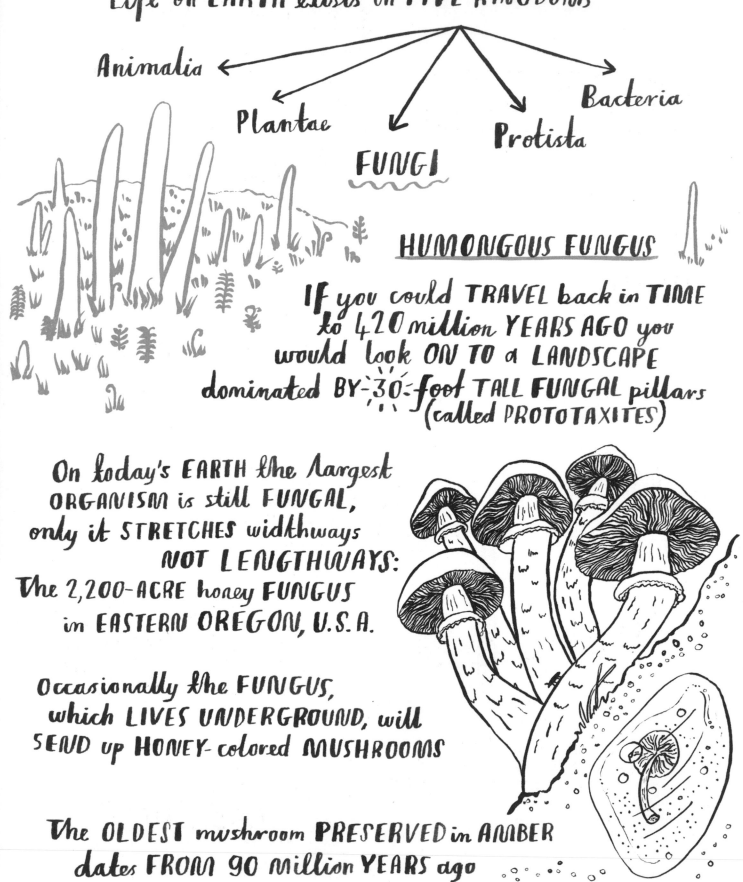

HUMONGOUS FUNGUS

If you could TRAVEL back in TIME to 420 million YEARS AGO you would look ON TO a LANDSCAPE dominated BY 30-foot TALL FUNGAL pillars (called PROTOTAXITES)

On today's EARTH the largest ORGANISM is still FUNGAL, only it STRETCHES widthways NOT LENGTHWAYS: The 2,200-ACRE honey FUNGUS in EASTERN OREGON, U.S.A.

Occasionally the FUNGUS, which LIVES UNDERGROUND, will SEND up HONEY-colored MUSHROOMS

The OLDEST mushroom PRESERVED in AMBER dates FROM 90 million YEARS ago

FUNGI is the PLURAL of FUNGUS, which IS an ORGANISM that feeds ON ORGANIC matter AND reproduces THROUGH SPORES

GERMINATION OF A SPORE

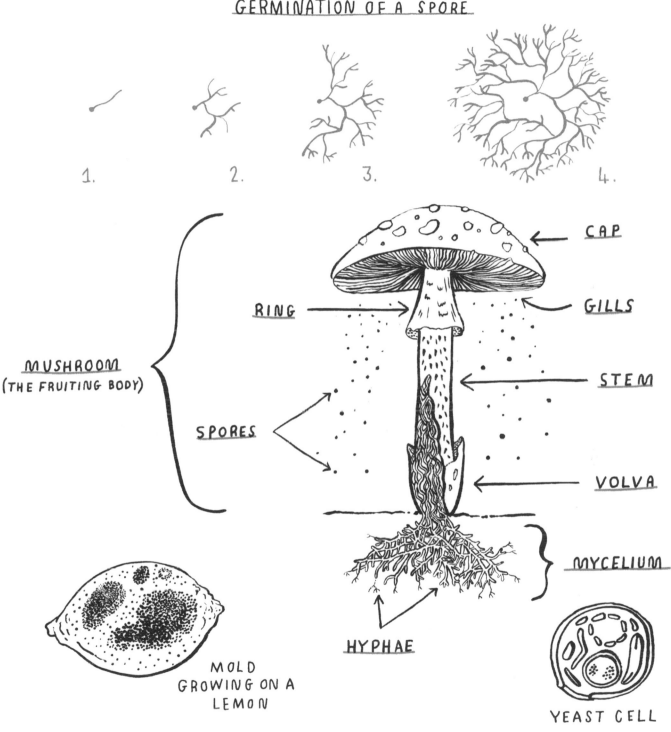

1.

2.

3.

4.

CAP

GILLS

RING

MUSHROOM
(THE FRUITING BODY)

STEM

SPORES

VOLVA

MYCELIUM

MOLD
GROWING ON A
LEMON

HYPHAE

YEAST CELL

There are 75,000 identified SPECIES of FUNGI.
COMMON types include MOLD, MUSHROOMS, and
single-celled ORGANISMS SUCH as YEAST

JOIN UP the hyphae in between the GERMINATING SPORES to FORM a SUPER STRUCTURE of INTERCONNECTING MYCELIA

When YOU'VE finished, TAKE A MOMENT
to ADMIRE HOW very BEAUTIFUL MYCELIA are —
ONE of the HIDDEN wonders of the WORLD

KNOW YOUR FUNGI

GILL FUNGI

THIS type OF FUNGUS has GILLS on the UNDERSIDE of THE CAP. Millions OF SPORES line THE densely PACKED GILLS and FLOAT DOWN when READY to START a NEW LIFE.

POLYPORES

Polypores often GROW OUT of TREE TRUNKS and ROTTING wood, although SOME may GROW on SOIL.
These FUNGI have SPORE-RELEASING pores ON the UNDERSIDE of THEIR caps AND PLAY a VERY important PART in FOREST ECOSYSTEMS as they HELP DECOMPOSE dead wood AND PLANT MATTER.

STINKHORNS

Stinkhorns GROW out of A STRUCTURE that LOOKS like AN EGG. SOME grow A LACY VEIL that HANGS down FROM the CAP. The HEAD of THE FUNGUS is COVERED with A SMELLY, sticky, SPORE-LADEN SLIME. Flies and OTHER INSECTS are ATTRACTED to THE rotten SMELL and help THE FUNGUS by CARRYING off THE spores TO new HABITATS.
Pretty INGENIOUS, DON'T YOU THINK??!

PUFFBALLS, EARTHSTARS, and EARTHBALLS

These FUNGI contain their SPORES inside a BALL which SPLITS OPEN when IT IS TIME for THEM to be released. WEIRD and amazing

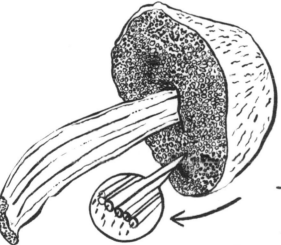

BOLETES

Boletes HAVE thousands of PORES RATHER than GILLS on THE underside OF THEIR CAPS, making them LOOK like SPONGES. EACH PORE is the TIP OF a tiny TUBE that RUNS vertical TO the CAP AND from WITHIN which SPORES come TUMBLING OUT.

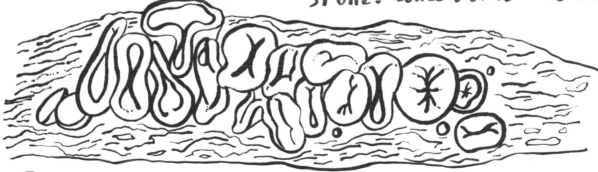

JELLY FUNGI

These FASCINATING fungi ARE RUBBERY, look LIKE BLOBS of CRINKLY JELLO, and GROW on TREES and ON THE GROUND.

DRAW a strange and beautiful
MUSHROOM FOREST

PATTERN is EVERYWHERE in NATURE

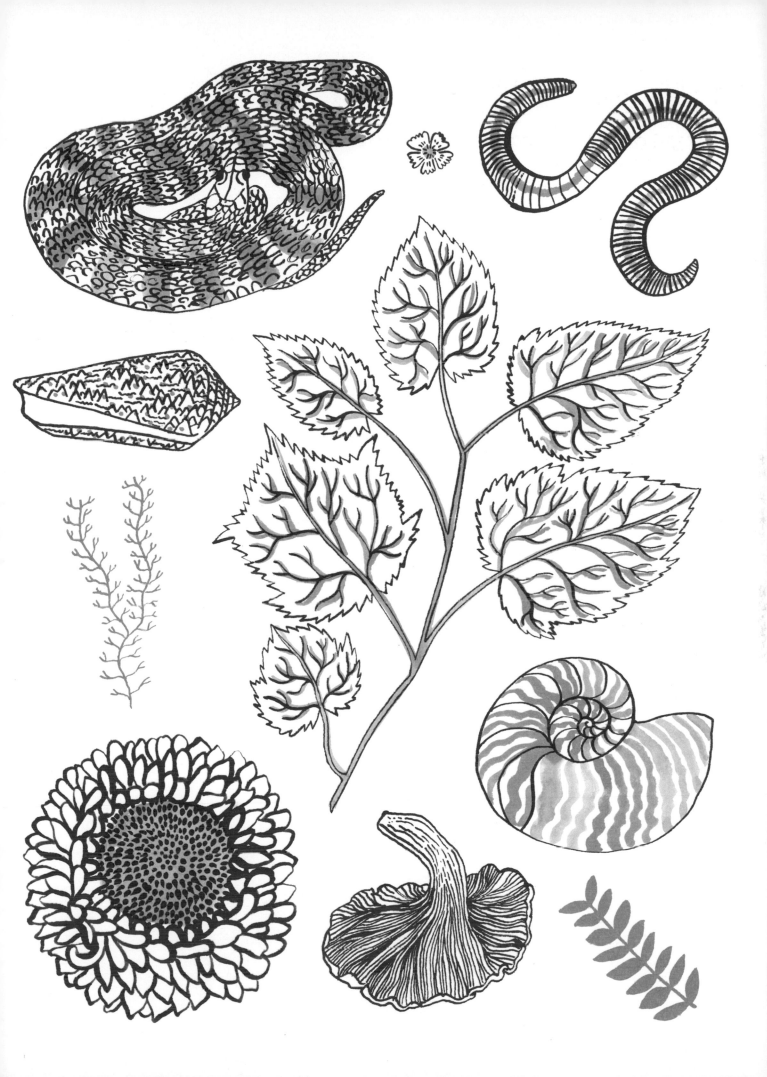

FILL these PAGES
with patterns YOU have
NOTICED in NATURE

It could
be a LEAF,
a seashell,
OR a FLOWER

It could BE
a feather,
an EGG, or
a STONE

If it's too COLD or RAINY to GO OUTSIDE collecting plants... then just draw them instead

DRAW some flowers on this page

DRAW some leaves on this page

The pigment (called CHLOROPHYLL) that keeps the
leaves GREEN starts to fade in fall
and MELLOW YELLOWS and WARM ORANGES
start to emerge

SELECT a beautiful fall leaf and
stick it down CAREFULLY on this page

ROLL ON FALL!
Write a list of all the things you LOVE about fall

USE WARM RED

PAINT *these* LEAVES
BEAUTIFUL FALL COLORS

USE DEEP PURPLE

USE
CHESTNUT
BROWN

USE
MELLOW
YELLOW

USE
FIERY
ORANGE

MAKE LEAF
PRINTS
(IT'S EASY...and FUN)

YOU WILL NEED:

INK

LEAVES

BRUSHES

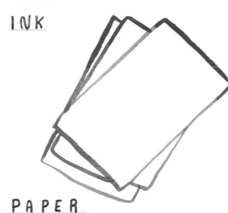

PAPER

Use fresh leaves, NOT dried ones as they tend to crumble

① Paint the leaves with ink and then PRESS them CAREFULLY on to a sheet of PAPER

Leo Tolstoy
WAR
and
PEACE

② Place another piece of paper ON TOP and weigh down with a HEAVY BOOK

③ After a minute or TWO, lift up the BOOK, the TOP sheet of paper, and the leaf to REVEAL your PRINT

Draw leaves on these PAGES
by PRESSING them FLAT on to the paper
and going round the outline with a
colored PEN or PENCIL

DRAW in the RIBS and VEINS of the leaves or, if you like the shapes, just COLOR them in

Fill these pages with YOUR leaf prints

Hibernating animals

FROSTY

SPIKY BRANCHES

ICY DAYS

Making snowmen

Holly

HELLO

COLD

DECIDUOUS TREES

SNOWFLAKES

WINTRY WALKS

COZY AFTERNOONS

Feeding hungry birds

CONIFERS

MIGRATING BIRDS

Icicles

Tracks in the snow

MISTLETOE

WINTER

Short days

SPIDER WEBS

Snowy nights

EVERGREEN TREES

Pine Cones

GUIDE to SNOWFLAKES

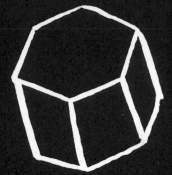

Simple Prisms

Bullet Rosettes

Simple Needles

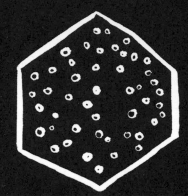

Rimed

12-Branched Stars

Crossed Needles

Graupel

Isolated Bullets

Fernlike Stellar Dendrites

Solid Columns

Simple Stars

Triangular Forms

Multiply Capped
Columns

Stellar Dendrites

Sheaths

Twin Columns

Hexagonal Plates

Needle Clusters

Irregulars

Radiating Dendrites

Stellar Plates

Arrowhead Twins

Crossed Plates

Radiating
Plates

FILL these PAGES WITH YOUR OWN SNOWFLAKES

MAKE each ONE
UNIQUE and WONDERFUL

DID you KNOW...?

NO TWO SNOWFLAKES are EXACTLY THE SAME

AN average SNOWFLAKE is MADE UP OF 180 BILLION MOLECULES of WATER

SNOWFLAKES are FORMED of ICE CRYSTALS

SNOW is A MINERAL, LIKE SALT or DIAMONDS

DRAW what YOU SEE

It's WINTERTIME and it's snowing.
What's on your horizon...?

DRAW the SPIDER
SPINNING
its WEB

If you bash into the WEB of a SPIDER, she DOESN'T get MAD. She WEAVES and REPAIRS it — Louise Bourgeois FRENCH-AMERICAN ARTIST

DRAW a WEB
so that this SPIDER
can REACH its DINNER on the OTHER PAGE

DID you KNOW...?
Spider silk is THE
strongest NATURAL FIBER known
and cannot be dissolved in water

DECIDUOUS TREES shed ALL their LEAVES
over the COLD, WINTER MONTHS

Draw a deciduous tree in WINTER
ON this page

EVERGREEN TREES, like most CONIFERS, keep their leaves all through winter

DRAW an evergreen tree on this page

DRAW the TOP HALF OF THIS
Sitka Spruce TREE

AN EVERGREEN TREE, the SITKA SPRUCE
KEEPS its LEAVES ALL YEAR ROUND

FILL this PAGE WITH DRAWINGS
OF PINE CONES and ACORNS

DRAW the OTHER HALF OF THIS Ash TREE

In SUMMER, TREES grow A LOT OF LEAVES in ORDER TO absorb AS MUCH SUNLIGHT as POSSIBLE

DRAW the OTHER HALF OF THIS
Horse Chestnut TREE

HEDGEHOGS can have up to ·5000· spines

Draw lots and lots of SPIKY SPINES
onto this HEDGEHOG

DRAW a BUSHY tail
on to this squirrel
and color it GRAY

SQUIRRELS live in trees
and collect NUTS for the winter

DRAW BUSHY tails
on to these squirrels
and color them RED

Some ANIMALS go into a DEEP SLEEP in winter called HIBERNATION.

Hibernation HELPS the animal to conserve ENERGY during the COLD, winter months when food is scarce

DRAW a HIBERNATING CREATURE on this page

HURRAH for WINTER!
WRITE a LIST of ALL the THINGS YOU LOVE ABOUT WINTER

OPEN A BIRD RESTAURANT

When it is cold OUTSIDE and BIRDS get very HUNGRY, you can HELP them out BY opening a BIRD RESTAURANT

YOU WILL NEED:

- a PLASTIC bottle (1 LITER)
- 2 STICKS (about 12 in long)
- Nail and HAMMER
- Garden String (16-24 in long)
- BIRD FOOD

① Wash the BOTTLE and peel off the LABEL

② Using the NAIL and HAMMER, punch two small HOLES opposite EACH OTHER near the BOTTOM of the bottle

③ Insert ONE of the STICKS so that it passes through one HOLE and out of the hole ON the OTHER SIDE

④ Punch out TWO MORE holes a little above THE FIRST perch but on the OPPOSITE side of the bottle AND insert the second stick INTO THE HOLES

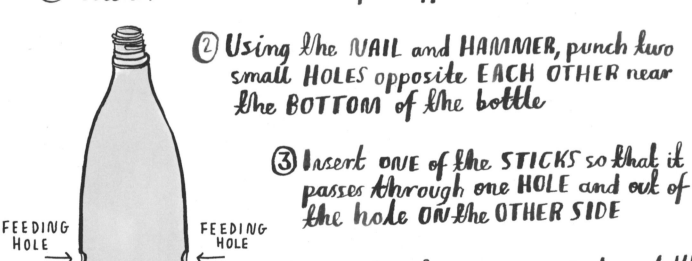

FEEDING HOLE → ← FEEDING HOLE

⑤ NOW make feeding HOLES: using the NAIL and HAMMER again MAKE a small hole above each PERCH. Keep the HOLES small or THE food will FALL OUT

⑥ Make two more HOLES at THE TOP of the bottle just under the rim, thread the STRING THROUGH and tie a FIRM KNOT at the TOP. You could double UP to ENSURE that THE STRING WILL be strong enough TO HOLD the FEEDER when it is FULL

⑦ Using a FUNNEL, carefully fill YOUR BIRD FEEDER with SEEDS, NUTS, and other TIDBITS

⑧ SCREW the CAP on and HANG the BIRD restaurant FROM a TREE branch outside YOUR WINDOW

Complete the drawing of THE BIRD →

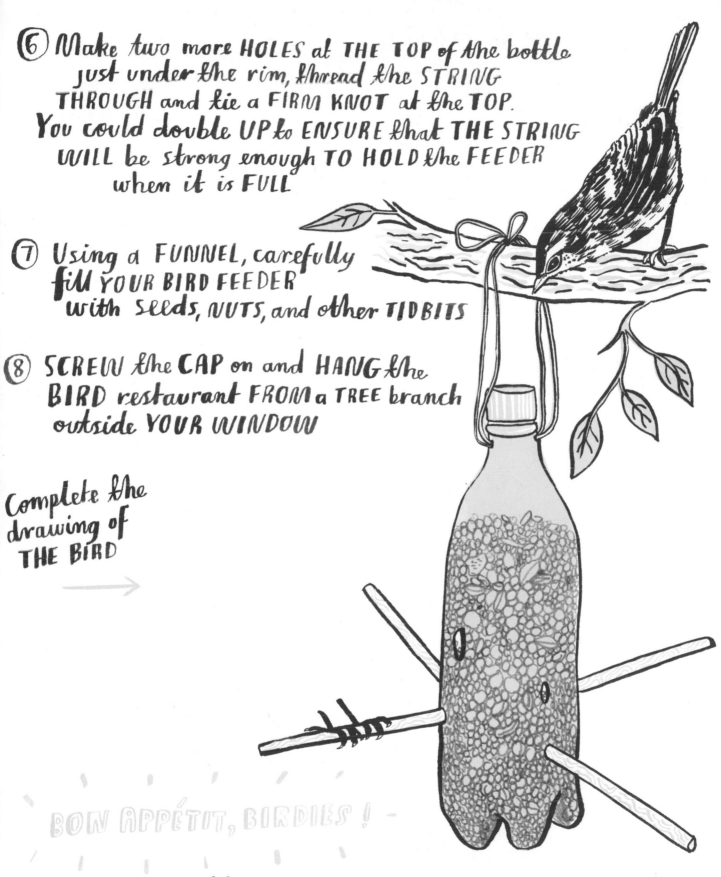

BON APPÉTIT, BIRDIES!

* DON'T forget to keep the restaurant CLEAN and WELL STOCKED

SEE NEXT PAGE FOR MENU IDEAS →

THE HAPPY BIRD RESTAURANT

MENU

✻ Delicious! SUNFLOWER

APPLE CORES Seeds

Nuts (UNSALTED) ✭ OATS ✭

✱ COOKED RICE ✳

Raw ✴ COCONUT PIECES

PASTRY CRACKED

SOAKED • Corn

DRIED FRUITS ∘∘◉◉◉◘

◆ GET THE BEST • FORGET THE REST ◆

WHEN BIRDS start VISITING
YOUR RESTAURANT,
     draw QUICK sketches
          of THEM ON THIS PAGE

'Orbiting EARTH in the spaceship,
I SAW how
BEAUTIFUL our planet is.
PEOPLE, let us
PRESERVE and INCREASE
this BEAUTY, NOT destroy it.'

—Yuri Gagarin
(1934–1968)

Russian astronaut and
FIRST person in space

On this PAGE
write a FANTASTIC poem
about nature

THANK YOU!

Laurence King, Jo Lightfoot, Angus Hyland, Melissa Danny, Elizabeth Jenner, Alex Coco, and Marianne Taylor

N.C.

2016

Extra-special thanks

to Emma Sullivan for inspirational early research and ideas, and to Ben Branagan for invaluable assistance and endless patience.